DELAWARE
Two Hundred Years Ago:
1780-1800

DELAWARE
Two Hundred Years Ago:
1780-1800

We The People
Delaware
••••• ♦ •••••
Freedom's First

Harold B. Hancock

A Delaware Heritage Commission book, commemorating the ratification of the United States Constitution

Publication made possible through a grant from The National Society of The Colonial Dames of America in the State of Delaware

THE MIDDLE ATLANTIC PRESS
Wilmington, Delaware

COVER ILLUSTRATION

This illustration of the Sussex County election riots in Lewes, Delaware on October 15, 1787 was painted in 1986 by Peggy Kane. The Division of Historical and Cultural Affairs of the Delaware Department of State commissioned this 6' 6" × 8' 2" painting for a special bicentennial exhibit entitled "Constitution Documents of the First State." The exhibit is on display at the Visitors Center in Dover, Delaware from December 1986 through December 1987.

DELAWARE TWO HUNDRED YEARS AGO: 1780–1800

A MIDDLE ATLANTIC PRESS BOOK

Copyright © 1987 Harold B. Hancock

A Delaware Heritage Commission book,
commemorating the ratification of the
United States Constitution by Delaware, "The First State"

Published with the Assistance of The National Society
of The Colonial Dames of America in the State of Delaware

First Middle Atlantic Press printing, September 1987

Library of Congress Cataloging-in-Publication Data

Hancock, Harold Bell, 1913–1987
    Delaware two hundred years ago.

    Bibliography: p. 212
    Includes index.
    1. Delaware—History.   2. Delaware—Social life
and customs.   I. Delaware Heritage Commission.   II. Title.
III. Title: Delaware 200 years ago.
F168.H36   1987   975.1'03   87-9123
ISBN 0-912608-52-8

The Middle Atlantic Press, Inc.
848 Church Street
Wilmington, Delaware

Manufactured in the United States of America

CONTENTS

ILLUSTRATIONS

PREFACE

In honor of the framing of the federal Constitution in Philadelphia in 1787 and of Delaware being the first state to ratify it, I decided to prepare a volume describing life in the state two hundred years ago, stressing its social, cultural, and political history. Intentionally I have prepared a popular study of that age, with many illustrations from newspapers, hoping that the volume would be enjoyed by adults and high school students. Emphasis is placed upon the 1780s and the early 1790s. For scholars I have prepared footnotes, which may be consulted in the Historical Society of Delaware and in the Delaware State Archives.

In connection with this study, I enjoyed the assistance and cooperation of many persons: in the Delaware State Archives, Dr. John Kern, Roy Tryon, Joanne Mattern, Russell McCabe, Doris Carignan, and Sherrie Ayers; in the Historical Society of Delaware, Dr. Barbara Benson, Dr. Constance Cooper, and Lyn Stallings; and at the Hagley Library, B. Bright Low, Marjorie McNinch, and Heddy Richter. Lyn Stallings and Lynn Ellen Peterson performed the tedious task of photographing most of the illustrations. Suggestions about the narrative were offered by Dr. George Frick, Dr. Barbara Benson, Dr. John A. Munroe, and Dr. William H. Williams. Dr. Claudia Bushman offered advice and encouragement. Dr. Bernard Herman, Assistant Director of the Center for Historic Architecture and Engineering, College of Urban Affairs and Public Policy, University of Delaware, provided information about the style of life and architecture. The manuscript benefited from the editorial expertise of Marjorie McNinch. Ruth Crossan typed several versions of the manuscript.

The exhibition "Delaware in the 1780s," mounted by the Historical Society of Delaware, was largely based on the manuscript of this book.

For illustrations I used material in the Historical Society of Delaware, Hagley Museum and Library, Wilmington Library, University of Delaware Archives, Massachusetts Historical Society and Delaware State Archives. All newspaper illustrations are from the collection of the Historical Society of Delaware.

Publication is made possible by the cooperation of the Colonial Dames of America, Delaware Chapter, and of the Delaware Heritage Commission.

September 1, 1986   Harold Hancock

Map ca. 1795. Delaware from the Best Authorities, Philadelphia. Engraved for Carey's. Courtesy of the Hagley Museum and Library. (following page)

I ———————————————— PRELUDE

Many Delawareans predicted that sunshine and prosper- ity, the beginning of a new era, would come with the arrival of peace with Great Britain. Instead they encountered frustrations, disappointment, and hardships. Everything seemed to be in a state of flux. Farmers saw their property being sold to meet their debts at a fraction of its real worth. Paper money declined in value in relation to specie until 1785, when the state called in the paper money issued in the past and redeemed it at the rate of seventy-five to one in new bills. Clashes between political parties intensified, resulting in both verbal and physical abuse. The governments of the state and of the nation seemed unable to deal with the prob- lems before them. Was there any hope? Would the United States fall apart and again become part of the British Empire?

During the 1780s many of these problems were solved, in part or whole. A gradual rise in the price of grain aided farmers. Paper money was placed on a sounder basis than it had been during the Revolution. Physical combat at elections was replaced by partisan speeches, pamphlets, and letters to the editors of newspapers. Steps were taken to ameliorate the lot of slaves and encourage manumissions. Both the nation and state received new constitutions to provide more effective government. By the 1790s, Fourth of July orators were prais- ing America as the promised land.

How these changes came about is an interesting story, which requires attention to such things as the composition of

1

the population, class structure, farming, manufacturing, religion and education, political parties, the ratification of the federal constitution, and the framing of a new state constitution. In brief, the narrative of these events is a biography of the people of Delaware and of the state's history during troubled times.

Since Dr. John A. Munroe wrote a comprehensive history of Federalist Delaware, in 1954, most of these topics, with a few exceptions, have been neglected. Hagley fellows have explored manufacturing and shipping. Dr. William H. Williams has written a lively history of the growth of Methodism in the Delmarva Peninsula at the end of the eighteenth century. Dr. Claudia Bushman and Dr. Harold Hancock have studied political and legislative history. Dr. Bernard Herman, Madeline Dunn Hite, and James Stewart are studying the style of life and architecture. Dr. Munroe has prepared a history of the University of Delaware. But topics in this period such as black history, the role of women, public and private education, transportation, denominational history except for the Methodists and Episcopalians, and the history of towns need attention. Let us hope that the Bicentennial honoring the ratification of the Constitution will bring forth new studies, as did the celebration of the American Revolution.

This volume demonstrates the need for such studies and provides evidence that material exists for useful monographs in many areas.

II ——————————— THE PEOPLE

Delaware is a small state, being only one hundred miles long and from nine to thirty-five miles wide. It is composed of three counties with the good English names of New Castle, Kent, and Sussex. Delaware's surface is relatively flat except for some hills north of the Christiana Creek in New Castle County. The eastern side of the state is indented with a large number of short creeks or rivers leading into the Delaware Bay or River, while the Nanticoke River in southwestern Sussex County flows into the Chesapeake Bay. These streams have been important for transportation and for fishing. The soil is well suited for agriculture. The only mineral exploited before the Revolution was iron from Iron Hill near Newark and from the bogs of Sussex County. Timber, especially in Sussex County, was an important resource.

When the Swedes arrived in 1638, they encountered Indians called the Lenni Lenape settled in small groups along the Christiana River. They engaged in hunting, fishing, and raising corn, squashes, and pumpkins. The Lenni Lenape were under frequent attack from the Iroquois Indians. In southwestern Sussex County the Nanticoke Indians lived along the stream of that name. By the middle of the eighteenth century another group of Indians were living along Indian River Inlet in Sussex County. But prior to the Revolution, most of these native Americans had disappeared, driven westward by the advance of white settlers. Some remained behind in pockets, especially along the Indian River, where their descendants are still living today. Recently, attention to their heritage has been revived by the formation of an Indian association.

The population of the state in 1775 was estimated to be composed of thirty-five thousand white inhabitants and two thousand black. But in view of the census returns of 1790, these figures, especially of the black population, are too low.

By 1782 the population had probably grown to be about 50,000 and in the census of 1790 had reached 59,096, almost equally divided among the three counties.

Population in 1790

	White	Slave	Free Black
New Castle	16,487	2,562	639
Kent	14,050	2,300	2,570
Sussex	15,773	4,025	690
	46,310	8,887	3,899

In the 1780s, most of the population of the state was of British descent. The small number of Dutch and Swedish

IRISH PASSENGERS EXPRESS APPRECIATION
FOR A SAFE VOYAGE
Delaware Gazette,
July 4, 1789

WE, the paſſengers, redemptioners, and ſervants, in all one hundred and ſeventy, from Belfaſt to America, take this pleaſing opportunity of returning our hearty and ſincere thanks to James Jefferis, maſter of the brig Brothers, for his unprecedented care and humanity to every perſon on board ; likewiſe for abundance of all ſorts of proviſion diſtributed moſt liberally: We therefore warmly recommend him to his country for the above, and to our friends in Ireland, as a captain adapted in every degree equal to carry on the paſſenger trade.

Signed by the following paſſengers:
Capt. Henry Hughes, William MᶜCluney, Sampſon Toft, John Denſmew, Samuel Scott, Andrew Davidſon, William Crabb, Francis Hamilton, William Huſton, John Walters, Jeremiah Walters, Patrick Waters, Thomas Hughes, John Hughes, Thomas Huſton, John

rrived in this port from New-Orleans, r sells at that place, at the rate of barrel.

provisions in Canada, and in the back k and Pennsylvania, mentioned, in apers, is owing chiefly to accidental a, the royal issues of provisions to the fore the persons fed by them had d in the new counties of New-York the accession of settlers has been so ond the supplies in provisions of those The scarcity is therefore both local t is expected that it will be wholly t, in the new lands of New-York and agazines of provisions being provided the accommodation of new settlers, ncrease of farms which are now un- a the East Branch of the Susquehan-

ays a correspondent, require not only but encouraging counties. In Scot- r is distributed in premiums for the support of manufactures. Near xpended in 20 years in Ireland, and granted annually in England for the ae congress of the United States shall of the above-mentioned countries, ble to give extent or permanency to ctures. 10 cool. a year appropriated buld be more profitable to four coun- of Peru. The duty upon only a fin- mposts would produce this sum, and a as much pleasure as the taxes for ernment, or the maintainance of the nd orphans, who gave their services s to the United States.

nington, July 4. arrived here the brig Brothers, Capt. s from Belfast, with 170 passengers, at in lat. 40 long. 53:30 they fell in ck, which he at the same time picked square rigged vessel, fore top-mast, cap of the fore-mast, with all the halliards, chair-plates, dead-eyes, pearance, suppofes her to be an Eu-

we have received the following In- telligence.

We have accounts from Geneva, ris, that the famous aristocracy, in- ears, is entirely put an end to, the d means to get possession of the entire arms they used to oppose the troops nes of the city, from whence they diers with boiling oil mixt with salt- y which out of 9000 men only 4000 ens do military duty, and the arif- sent couriers to Versailles, Turin t the assistance of those three powers, of the treaty of 1782; in the mean e quiet, after having proved that no pose the courage of a people strug- ty.

[DONDERRY.

McFadden, William Wier, Joseph Dearman, Henry Dearmon, Archibald Conner, Samuel Thompson, Robert Ross, William Ross, Nathan Gregg Bryson, Samuel Patton, Alexander McKinnon, John Tamison, Adam Boal, Leonard Paisley, Daniel Carr, William McCune, Robert Wallace, Henry O'Hagan, John Livingston, Henry Morgan, James McCulloch, Thomas Latherdale, James Caughroggs, David Crockbanks, William O'Connel, Adam Murdoch, Hugh Girvin, John McGowan, John Gordon, Alexander Clark, William Adams, David McGerrald, William Blair, Robert Carolon, John Carolon, James Armstrong, Joseph Tosh, George Kenne- dy, James Rodgers, James Mulhollan, John Brannan, Jacob Corsby, William Corsby, Henry Montgomery, William Castlin, John Huston, William Bell, Robert Smith, Thomas Watson, Samuel Linton, William Moony, John Bell, Matthew Brown, William Martin, and Hugh Strickland.

The following Encomium was composed by a young gentleman who came as passenger in the above brig, and inserted at the request of a number of his fellow passengers.

On the Brig Brothers, James Jefferis, master.

1.

YOU valiant hearted countrymen, of every degree, If resolved to make a fortune, pray listen unto me; To brave captain Jefferis, my lads you must appeal, On board the brig Brothers, just ready for to sail.

2.

The seventh day of May, in the year eighty-nine, Bound for the land of Freedom we left Belfast behind; With passengers in number, with pleasure we do tell, One hundred and seventy, all landed safe and well.

3.

When on the western ocean this vessel she did steer, All passengers were merry with excellent good cheer; The can of grog we pushed about, with bumpers flowing (o'er, Toasting our friends and sweethearts left on the Irish (shore.

4.

She is as safe a vessel as ever cross'd the main, The captain who commands her, all fear he does disdain; The regulation kept on board, with victualling also, Exceedeth any other that in that trade doth go.

5.

In Wilmington we landed; for a tavern did enquire, To toast our noble captain, by all the crew's desire; The natives they came crowding in, our merry men to (see, To welcome us as Irishmen, just landed from the sea.

6.

Now all you trading captains pray warning take by this, Ne'er let your passengers complain, or say you do amiss; A pattern pray you take by what we here set forth, Brave Jefferis can instruct you, as well we know his worth.

7.

Of Washington we often read, ever noted for his fame, Vast armies having conquered upon his native plain; Our worthy hero we compare unparallel'd in his station, To generals and captains all of every foreign nation.

Extract of a letter from Charleston, dated June 20. "Georgia is now in the greatest distress; urge con- gress to something soon, or the state is lost; the Indians have acted a treacherous part, and were we in a situa-

settlers in the seventeenth century left behind few traces—
only the names of families such as Stidham, Stalcop, Springer,
Justice, Van Dyke, and Vandergrift, and physical features
such as the Christiana and Murderkill rivers. Another heritage was Old Swedes Church.

New Castle County contained the most varied population,
being the home of more persons of Dutch and Swedish
descent than were in the other two counties. The majority of the
inhabitants were of English descent. The Scotch-Irish migrat-
ing from northern Ireland formed a strong minority, as the
presence of numerous Presbyterian churches indicates. The
town of New Castle was a favorite landing place for these
immigrants. Many traveled on into Pennsylvania, but some
stayed in Delaware. Sometimes the passengers were so grate-
ful for a safe voyage that they presented to the captain a

REWARDS OFFERED FOR RUNAWAY SLAVES

Delaware Gazette, May 16, 1789, July 18, 1789, October 9, 30, 1790.
(following pages)

paid by

WILLIAM ELLIOT, jun.

July 9, 1789.

Three Pounds Reward.

RAN away on the 9th of July laſt a negro lad called STEPHEN--he is a very black fellow, and about 5 feet 9 or 10 inches high, about 24 or 25 years of age, and was brought up to the blackſmith buſineſs, at which he is tolerable good and alſo fond of --he is tolerable well ſet, has remarkable yellow eyes, has loſt an upper tooth before, chews tobacco, & is fond of ſtrong liquors, & when drunk is very talkative--he is a good reaper, took his ſickle with him, and will probably reap this harveſt--he can alſo cradle. His clothes were, a ſmall half-worn fur Hat, a coarſe grey cloth Coat of foreign manufacture, an old cloth Jacket with londonbrown fore-parts, and deep blue back-parts, half worn ſatinnet Jacket and Breeches, half worn nankeen Trowſers, new tow Shirt and Trowſers, half worn fine linen Shirt, and half worn Shoes with odd Buckles. It is ſuppoſed he has got a paſs, ſo well drawn that it will deceive, if not attentively examined, and will ~all himſelf *Stephen Miller* or *Stephen Gibbs*. I have reaſon to believe that he will make for the upper part of Cheſter county. Jerſey or New-York. Whoever will ſecure him in any goal, ſo that his owner may get him again, ſhall be entitled to the above Reward ; or it brought to the ſubſcriber living in the upper part of Little-Creek hundred, Kent county, Delaware, ſhall be paid reaſonable charges.

ditto, Harlem Oil, Wham Bateman's Drops, Daffy's Elixir, frey's Cordial, Turlington's Bal Life, &c. &c.

The following

BLANK

are to be ſold at this Printing-Offi

Judgment Bonds

Plain do.

Judgment Notes

Mortgage Deeds

Bills of Lading

Apprentices Indentures

Arbitration Bonds

Powers of Attorney, &c. &

Juſt imported in the Brig Brothers Belfaſt,

BRISTOL & Belfaſt 8 by 10 dow-Glaſs

EIGHT DOLLARS Reward.

RAN away *from Elk Forge, Cæcil county, Maryland, on the 23d inſtant, a* Negro Man named ZACK, *about 20 years of of age, and 6 feet or more high --- Had on, when he went away, a tow ſhirt and trowſers, a ſmall wool hat, blue cloth jacket without ſleeves, and not any ſhoes. He may change his clothes and name, and probably endeavour to paſs for a free man. Whoever takes up ſaid Negro, and ſecures him in any gaol, ſo that his maſter may have him again, ſhall receive the above reward if fifty or more miles from home, and* Six Dollars *if leſs than fifty, and reaſonable charges if brought home.* THOMAS JOHNS.

N. B. *All maſters of veſſels and others are forbid to harbour or carry off ſaid Negro at their peril.*

Auguſt 27, 1789.

New-Caſtle county ſs.

BY virtue of an order of the Orphans Court for the

which the m mined for an paſt, preſent, ation of the latitude being is alſo eaſily a quarter of land, which i ations of the deceaſed, an geographers ; ral voyages r

The work by a very ref characters (v

JUST IMPORTED,

In the Schooner Pratt, a few Hhds. of RUM and SUGAR, the latter is of the firſt quality, and for Sale, by

JOSEPH SUMMERL.

Wilmington, May 23

TEN POUNDS Reward.

RAN AWAY from the ſub-ſcriber, living on Broad-creek, Suffex county and ſtate of Delaware, on the 6th Sept. laſt, a NEGROE MAN, named CÆSAR, nearly 6 feet high, ſtout and well made: he has a ſcar on one of his wriſts, which is much whiter than the reſt of his ſkin; and a ſcar on his noſe reſembling a pit of the ſmall pox: he has a large beard, a ſtern and ſurly look, and is very ſhort in his anſwers to queſtions aſked him. Had on when he went away, a light brown furtout coat, claret colored coat, blue and white ſtriped linſey waiſtcoat, red and white chequered trowſers, and an old hat turned almoſt yellow. Whoever takes up the ſaid Negroe, and ſecures him, ſo that his maſter may have him again, ſhall receive *Five Pounds,* but if lodged in Dover Gaol, or brought home, then the above reward.   **FRANCIS L. GODDARD.**

May 16, 1789.

---

eward.

iber, living
ounty, Ma-
laſt, a NE-
e is a ſtout
ears of age,
gh, he was
marks of it
breaſt and
on when he
rt and trow-
reeches of a
s and ſhoes,
er takes up
his maſter

Notice.

WAS taken up in this county, on Friday night laſt, a negro man who calls himſelf Harry. a ſmart young fellow, he had on him a lappelled linſey coat, of a browniſh caſt, with white metal buttons, blue and white ſtriped trowſers, and felt hat, he rode a ſmart bay mare, with a ſtar in her forehead, and trots; there was a ſaddle & bridle on ſaid mare; the negro I have lodged in gaol, and the mare I have in poſſeſſion. Whoever proving property and paying charges, may have the above. by applying to

Patrick M'Cormick

New-Caſtle Oct. 30.   3w   92

Treaſury Department, Sep. 28, 1790.

NOTICE is hereby given, that propoſals will be re-

For Sale—Twenty Negroes
At Middletown

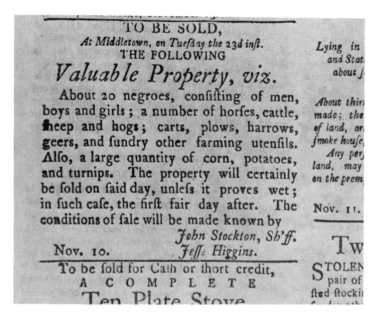

Delaware Gazette, November 13, 1790.

statement or verses of appreciation, as did those of the *Keziah* and *Brothers* in 1789. A few Scots were mixed in with the population. A communal settlement of Welsh lived on a tract of land near Newark. Following an insurrection in Santo Domingo in the 1790s, a wave of French-speaking people arrived in Wilmington.

Kent and Sussex counties were inhabited mainly by people of English descent, with names like Mitchell, Dickinson, Smith, Collins, and Ridgely. Many of the inhabitants, such as the Chew, Ridgely, and Dickinson families, had migrated there from nearby Maryland counties, seeing an opportunity to acquire good land cheaply.

The typical male Delawarean in the 1780s was of English

Announced Annual Meeting
of a Wilmington Abollition Society

omer.

f the Prefi-
deferves for
thing tend-
ind worthy
inform the
CATO.

9
e following

il officers of

les, and for

unding bill,
pofe, of re-

ogether of a

rmining the
ive to fteam.
fhed.

q. prefident,
f the Dela-

neral affem-
lirecting the
ction for a
of the Uni-
he part of
prefident of

county aforefaid.
JAMES BOOTH, clk. Orphans court.
New-Caftle, Nov. 19, 1788.

THE members of the Delaware Society in Wilmington, for the gradual
abolition of flavery, and for the relief
and protection of free negroes and mu-
lattoes unlawfully held in bondage, or
otherwife oppreffed, are defired to take
notice, that this day at 2 o'clock,
P. M. is the time for their annual meeting to be held, at Solomon Fuffel's
School-houfe, for the election of a Prefident, Secretary, Treafurer, and part
of the acting committee, &c.

Any perfon inclining to become a
member, may have an opportunity of
feeing the conftitution, on applying to
the acting committee.

                    Edward Hewes,
                    John Yarnall,
                    Jofeph Warner,
                    Stephen Wilfon,
                    Jofhua Wollafton.
Wilmington, 1ft mo. 31, 1789.

Delaware Gazette, January 31, 1789.

descent, living with his wife and several children on a small
farm of thirty to one hundred acres. He had undoubtedly
served in the militia during the Revolution, and either he or a
neighbor had been involved in combat during the war in New
York, New Jersey or the South. Before the Revolution he
probably thought of himself as an Anglican, even though he
seldom attended services. Following the Revolution, he turned
to Methodism. If he lived in Sussex County during the war,

Rewards Offered for the Capture
Of Two Runaway Indentured Servants

merit, publici
et omnibus præ-
VASHINGTON,
m, non folum de
iam humano ge-
led, bello æque
pprefentiffimum,
ivem præftantif-
, patriæque pa-
itur, &c."

e.

ifs America, in
efpecially where
lies of wearing

ugly;" and I
hem on, might,
r name than the

S. Y.

may chooie to employ him will pleafe to give him notice, and they will be waited on, by
R O B E R T   C A R O L O N.

One Guinea Reward.

RAN away from on board the fhip St. James, lying at New-Caftle, an Irifh indented fervant man, named WILLIAM M'LANE, a weaver by trade; he is a fhort thick man, with black hair.--- Had on, a dark grey coat, white cloth breeches, blue woollen flockings, and fmall plain buckles in his fhees. Any perfon who will fecure him in any gaol, fo that I get him again, fhall receive the above reward.
JOSEPH WISLON.

New-Caftle, July 23, 1789.
N. B. All Captains of veffels are forewarned from taking him off at their peril.

Wilmington, July 23, 1789.
ARRIVED in this port, the brig Keziah, Robert Brown, Mafter, from Londonderry, in 8 weeks: I am

Delaware Gazette, July 25, 1789; July 10, 1790.

he was probably conservative in his political outlook. When national parties were formed in the 1790s, he became a Federalist.

By 1790 about one-fifth of the population was black, mostly slave. The ratio of slave to free was more than two to one, a figure that was to change rapidly in the next decades. Many slaves had been brought into Delaware from Maryland by their masters.

Economically the black population ranked on the lowest level. Most black inhabitants, whether slave or free, worked as domestics or as farm laborers, but a few were employed as watermen, teamsters, or blacksmiths. They lived in cabins, often sparsely furnished, and ate coarse food, though it was abundant. A few owned land and acquired enough of the world's goods to be taxed at a higher rate than some of their white neighbors.

Discrimination against black persons had appeared early in the eighteenth century when special "Negro Courts" were

THE NEGRO'S HYMN

O THOU! Who doest with equal eye
    All human kind survey,
And mad'st all nations of the earth
    From the same mass of clay:
If pity in thy nature dwell,
    Behold our race forlorn:
Behold us from our native soil,
    From wives, from children torn.

Chain'd in the ship's dark scanty womb,
    Behold us want for breath,
Envying those friends, who happier far,
    Exchange their bonds for death,
Behold us in the sun's fierce blaze
    Struggling with toil and pain.
Behold us sink beneath the last
    Expiring on the plain!
And who are they that dare torment.

The produce of thy hand,
And with their brethren's blood, like Cain,
    Pollute both sea and land?
Ah! 'tis a race that falsely boast
    Salvation through his name,
Who taught "What ye with men to do,
    Do ye to them the same."
Yet vengeance is not our request:
    We ask but LIBERTY;
And light sufficient to explore
    The way that leads to thee.
If these, in mercy, then bestow,
    O! may thy bounty move
Our hearts, our minds, our souls to glow,
    With gratitude and love!

The Columbian Almanac, 1793, n. p.

set up to hear their cases. The legislature placed restrictions on their owning firearms, and on their assembling in groups of more than six without the presence of a white person.

In the 1780s important changes were made in the laws governing slaves. The General Assembly forbade the sale of slaves into the state from overseas or outside of the state, stopped outfitting vessels to engage in the slave trade from Delaware ports, and made easier the manumission of slaves.

During the Revolution only white males in Delaware were permitted to join the militia or to enlist in the Delaware Regiment. But two black men from Delaware—"Jack" and Cato Fagin—according to records in the National Archives—did serve in the Continental Army. Upon at least one occasion in 1780, a committee of the legislature considered forming a black military company, as had been done in some other states, but they then rejected the idea.

Black inhabitants did contribute to American history through supplying the labor on plantations and the payment of taxes, but not through military service. With many of their masters away at war, black workers were needed to operate farms under the supervision of white family members. Black freedmen, along with their white neighbors, paid assessments in corn and wheat for the support of the Continental Army in 1780. And they also provided other services. Isaac Carty, Receiver of Supplies for Kent County, acknowledged this debt in his accounts in 1781 when he listed payments: to "Negro Jack" for several months of service, including express riding and superintending horses; to his own black men "in public service"; to "Negro Daniel"; to a "Negro man" employed by W.Z.F.; and to Jack Needham, "Negro." Richard Allen, who was later an important black religious leader, hauled salt from Lewes for the Continental Army.

In the eighteenth century, slaves and freedmen attended white churches. Before the Revolution, clergyman of the Church of England made special efforts to provide religious instruction for blacks. Later in the century, slaves and freedmen enjoyed the Methodist services with their lively hymn singing and emotional preaching. "Black Harry" Hosier, a traveling companion of Bishop Francis Asbury, was noted for his fine sermons. Richard Allen, a former slave in Kent County, became a Methodist and later founded a black church in Philadelphia, the African Methodist Episcopal Church. Absalom Jones of Sussex County joined the Episcopal Church and was the founder of St. Thomas Episcopal Church, the first black church of that denomination.

Advertisements for runaway slaves in Wilmington and Philadelphia newspapers in the 1780s indicate that a few of them could read and write, some could play the violin, and others had learned trades such as blacksmithing, carpentry, or shoemaking. In 1764, when John Dickinson advertised his plantation of two thousand acres in Kent County for rent, he mentioned that the tenant might wish to hire some of his slaves as tailors, shoemakers, tanners, carpenters, or farm laborers. In 1772 the owners of Unity Forge near the Nanticoke River in Sussex County claimed that slaves and black servants in their employ were skilled in working iron for blooming and refining.

Due to the work of Warner Mifflin, a Quaker abolitionist, and others, many blacks were being freed in Kent County in the 1770s and 1780s. In 1777 John Dickinson made arrangements to free thirty-seven slaves—twelve male, ten female, and fifteen children—upon completion of twenty-one years of service. The children were to be taught to read and write by the age of ten. By 1790, Delaware, the smallest slave state, had a higher percentage of free blacks in its population than any other state—6.6 percent of the total population. Kent County was the home of 2,500 free blacks, or sixty-six percent of the state's total. One student of black history (Elizabeth Moyne Homsey) believes that economic reasons, such as the lack of undeveloped land and declining yields from exhausted farms, became more important in explaining the large number of manumissions in Kent County than moral or religious reasons.

In 1785 a Quaker petition to the legislature gave another

reason why slaves should be freed: Since the Declaration of
Independence proclaimed that all men were created equal and
were endowed with the unalienable rights of life, liberty, and
the pursuit of happiness, the holding of persons in bondage
was unjustifiable. Therefore, steps for gradual abolition should
be taken by the Assembly.

The example of Pennsylvania inspired abolitionists in Delaware to form societies to work toward freeing slaves. The
Delaware Society for Promoting the Abolition of Slavery and
the Delaware Society for the Gradual Abolition of Slavery
were both organized in 1788. The members, who were mostly
Wilmington Quakers, protected freedmen from kidnapping
and encouraged slave owners to release their slaves. Their
hearts were probably touched by notices such as this from the
Delaware Gazette of 1795: "For Sale—A Negro wench and
two children, one a girl of two years old, the other a boy of
six years old. They will be sold separately or together as may
best suit the purchaser."

Some slaves became free under unusual circumstances. In
Sussex County, "Negro Joseph" bought the freedom of his
wife and children in 1792 for thirty pounds. Two years later,
"Negro Bedford" purchased his own freedom for fifty-six
pounds. In Kent County in 1797 James Summers freed his
own children.

Not all Delawareans favored abolition; many wished for
stricter control of freedmen and slaves. In 1785 a petition to
the legislature declared that there were many idle free Negroes and "evil-disposed" slaves strolling around the state
without passes. Some of the slaves had come from other
states and might become public charges. The petition recommended the passage of legislation forbidding Negroes to
travel from one county to another without passes and the
expulsion of freedmen who had come here from other states.

The manumission of slaves in larger numbers, whether for
moral, religious, or economic reasons, began in the 1780s.
While the General Assembly modified regulations concerning
slavery, the members could not agree upon abolition. Perhaps

some of them agreed with Thomas Rodney, who had once expressed the opinion that blacks were fated to be hewers of wood and manual laborers in a white society. But by 1860 only 1,798 slaves remained in the state, mostly living in Sussex County.

Another so-called minority group—though in reality they were the majority in numbers in the state in the 1780s—was women, and they had a long struggle ahead of them to equality in rights, privileges, and status. The figures in the state census of 1782 as well as in the national census of 1790 reveal that more women than men lived in Delaware. Orators frequently referred to women as "the fair sex" or "the weaker sex," but the Revolution revealed that they were capable of performing strenuous tasks. With their husbands away on militia duty or in the Continental Army, they were called upon to take charge of farms with the aid of indentured servants and slaves. In addition, the times necessitated that they exert themselves in other ways, such as in sewing for soldiers. When Thomas Rodney was Clothier General of the First Delaware Regiment in June, 1779, he recorded that nineteen women in Kent County had cut out and sewed 427 shirts. The record book of the state auditor frequently lists payment to women for services:

To Sarah Mason for expenses of Doctors, nurses and others and for funeral charges of burying her deceased husband. £15.16.10 ½.

To United States for expenses of Captain Curtis Kendall's party of 8 Virginia soldiers and a wash woman on their way to camp.

For an order in favor of Ann Westley for cooking for a party of soldiers and taking care of a sick prisoner sent on shore by the Saratoga man of war.

A like order in favor of Elizabeth Thompson for dieting soldiers of the Delaware Regiment.

To Elizabeth Townsend for provisions and liquor for 35 men and horse feeding in October, 1777.

The concept that women were fragile creatures, to be admired from afar, but not the equal of men seemed to be disappearing. In 1795 a young man wrote a tribute in a poem to "Miranda," praising her physical beauty, but in the last lines he expressed admiration for the beauty of her mind. In the 1790s some girls attended special schools, and others had the same instructors as boys. Thomas Dilworth, a Wilmington schoolmaster, in an essay upon the education of youth written in 1791 expressed the opinion that women could seldom spell, write, or cipher well. The reason, he thought, was very obvious: they did not remain in attendance long enough in "writing school," i.e. elementary school. "Girls therefore ought to be put to the writing school," he thought, "as early as boys, and continued in it as long, and then it may reasonably be expected that both sexes should be alike ready with their pen." In case of widowhood, educated women could then manage business affairs better. He concluded, "The woman who has had a liberal education this way knows the advantages that arise from the ready use of the pen; and the woman who has learnt little or nothing of it, cannot but lament the want of it." (See appendix for his essay.)

Women possessed few political and legal rights. They did not vote, sue in court, or, if married, own real estate. If their husbands died without a will, they were entitled to one-third of his estate. Unless a woman was a widow, she was always supposed to have a male for a protector, such as father, brother, or husband. Like males, women could be fined, jailed, whipped, and placed in stocks.

Most women in the state lived on farms and took an active part in performing chores. A Smithsonian publication entitled

After the Revolution, by Barbara Clark Smith, provides interesting information about the role of women in the Thomas Springer household in Mill Creek Hundred in New Castle County at the end of the eighteenth century. In the spring, women were responsible for planting gardens, which they kept weeded and hoed during the summer. They preserved fruits and vegetables in stone jars, and they dried herbs and fruits. They milked the cows twice a day and made butter for sale in nearby markets. They spun yarn from wool sheared from the family sheep, though weaving, fulling (tightening the weave and softening the finish), and dyeing were often performed by specialists. Flax was also raised and spun into yarn to be sent out to a weaver and dyer. From homespun woolen and linen cloth came household garments. Linen was also used for curtains, towels, and quilts.

Cooking was often conducted in an outside kitchen, which removed both confusion and heat from the main house. Here meals were prepared over fireplaces three times a day with the aid of hooks, spits, and Dutch ovens. In the summer, mutton, beef, poultry, and fish, along with homegrown vegetables, fruits, and berries were served, while in the winter salted and cured meat, especially pork, was a staple. The inventory of every Delaware farmer listed large quantities, sometimes several hundred pounds of bacon.

Large families were common in spite of a high mortality rate among children. Smith believed that women became pregnant about every two years. Women spent about twenty years in a cycle of bearing, nursing, and raising children. Infants were usually breast-fed for a year or longer, and sometimes a wet nurse was hired. Girls were useful in performing household duties, while boys were expected to assist their fathers in outside activities. Slaves, laborers, and indentured servants supplemented the work of family members.

A Fourth of July oration might seem an unlikely place for a tribute to women for their work during the Revolution and in raising their families, but Dr. James Tilton, respected revolutionary surgeon and President of the Society of Cincin-

A Poem In Praise Of Miranda

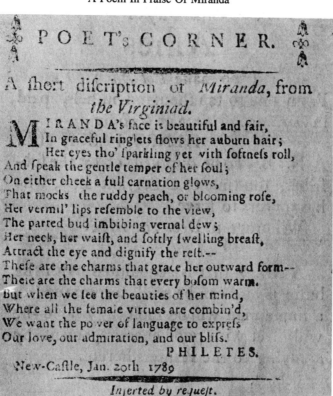

POET's CORNER.

A short discription of *Miranda*, from
the *Virginiad.*

MIRANDA's face is beautiful and fair,
In graceful ringlets flows her auburn hair;
  Her eyes tho' sparkling yet with softness roll,
And speak the gentle temper of her soul;
On either cheek a full carnation glows,
That mocks the ruddy peach, or blooming rose,
Her vermil' lips resemble to the view,
The parted bud imbibing vernal dew;
Her neck, her waist, and softly swelling breast,
Attract the eye and dignify the rest.--
These are the charms that grace her outward form--
These are the charms that every bosom warm.
But when we see the beauties of her mind,
Where all the female virtues are combin'd,
We want the power of language to express
Our love, our admiration, and our bliss.
                          PHILETES.
New-Castle, Jan. 20th 1789

Inserted by request.
MECHANIC's SONG.

Delaware Gazette, February 7, 1789.

nati, included a eulogy on women on that occasion in 1790.
His main points were that women had encouraged men to
fight for independence and that women were "equal in importance" to men in families because they controlled manners and morals. Some quotations follow from the quarter of
the speech that he devoted to women, some of whom were
sitting in the audience.

The men may boast of the strength of arm and supe-

A Wilmington Bookstore
Advertises the Rights Of Women

[NO. 69.

RIGHTS OF WOMEN.

JUST come to hand, and for sale, by THOMAS MARRIOTT, at his Shop, opposite the Lower Market-House—likewise at his Dwelling, opposite the Store lately occupied by George Clarke—

Rights of Woman	Ladies' Magazine
Family Bibles	Misses' do.
School do.	Rowe's Letters
Testaments & Primmers	Moore's Fables
Spelling-Books,	Dodsley's do.
Church Prayer-Books	Facetious Story of John
Psalm-Books	Gilpin
Gough's Arithmetick	Ready Reckoner
Dilworth's Book-keeping	Wild Oats
	Clark's Cæsar
Dyer's sermons, orChrist's	Davideis
famous Titles	The Builder's Pocket
Barclay's Catechism	Treasure, by W. Pain
Fisher's do.	Present for an Apprentice
Rise and Progress of Re-	Family Instructor
ligion in the Soul	Devil on Two Sticks
Sentimental Lucubra-	Dialogues of Devils
tions	Roderick Random
Schoolmaster's Assistant	Burns' Poems,
The Gamester	Family Physician
Seven Champions	Curiosities of Literature
Cullens's First Lines	Beauties of the Creation
Maria Cecilia	Denham's Poems
Juliet Grenville	Priestley's Remarks on
Sketches from Nature	Blackstone's Commen-
Fille de Chambre	taries
Sirets' French Grammar	Song-Books
Peter Pindar	American Revolution
Practical Farmer	Blind Child
Entick's Latin Diction-	Family Prayers
ary	Carey on the Fever
Sanford and Merton	Maghew's Sermons
Lippencott's Tables	

CHILDREN's BOOKS.

Harvey's Meditations	Merry and Wife
abridged	Monitor

(left margin fragments) ON and r wharf, sets out and Sa- : use of iblic no-

ely for a has spa- sengers; together

ived and vessel.— d, or to TON.

day of

Redlion upland, a large ood Ti- f it will s fertile marsh is of the ve view the ex- ts need

(right margin, vertical) Wanted, a Number of honest, steady Men, to be employed

The volume advertised was
probably Mary Wollstonecraft's
*A Vindication of the Rights of
Women* published in England in 1792.
Delaware Gazette, January 17, 1795.

rior authority; the women, under the modest term of influence, are of equal importance. The men possess the more ostensible powers of thinking and executing the laws; the women in every free country have an absolute control of manners: and it is confessed that in a republic manners are of equal importance with laws. I should therefore be uncandid, did I not on this occasion declare that for the manners of our country, our fair patriots are solely responsible.

All authority agrees in establishing the native influence and important duty of the mother:

To teach the young idea how to shoot [i.e. develop]. And you, my younger and fairest sisters, will be duly guarded against those seducing triflers, who tell you it is no matter what a woman says or does. Believe me, your very thoughts and opinions are of the utmost consequence to the public.

But it is with pleasure I acknowledge their native equality and dwell upon the fair prospect of perfecting the female character in this, our country. Here no austere religion shackles the mind; no tyrannic arm dare oppress the weaker sex. Their talents and their virtues have free course: *they may run and be glorified.*

His remarks about the role of women in society are so unusual for this period that a copy of this portion of his speech has been placed in the appendix.

In a similar vein, Captain Edward Roche at a Fourth of July observance in Dover in 1791, before the Society of Cincinnati, claimed that women drew men "from savage barbarity" into civilization, shaped "the plastic minds of the rising generation," and encouraged men to be patriots and honorable in their conduct.

Booksellers handled volumes and magazines of special interest to women. In 1794, a bold bookseller in Wilmington dared head one column of volumes for sale "Rights of Women," bringing to the attention of his customers a volume written by Mary Wollstonecraft in England. Also in 1794, Mathew Carey of Philadelphia advertised publications of his firm in a Wilmington newspaper, including some of special interest to women. For example, *The Young Misses Magazine,* in two volumes, contained "Dialogues between a governess and several young ladies of quality, her scholars—in which each lady is made to speak according to her particular genius, temperament and inclination— Their several faults are pointed out and the easy way to amend them, as well as how to think and speak and act properly; no less care being taken to form their hearts to goodness than to enlighten their understandings with careful knowledge." In brief, young ladies who read this magazine were being taught to speak, write, and think for themselves, not to be subservient to anyone, but to establish themselves as individuals.

One of the persons who petitioned for incorporation of the Library Company of Wilmington in 1788 was a woman, and that collection of books included several of special interest to women.

While most women in this period were homemakers, circumstances such as the American Revolution or widowhood sometimes forced them to be active in business or as managers of farms. Several women in Wilmington operated "fancy" stores or conducted schools for girls. Mrs. Sarah Kean of Wilmington was the proprietor of a grocery and dry goods store in 1793. Mrs. Clay of New Castle and Mrs. Battell of Dover conducted taverns. Following the death of her husband, Mrs. Ann Moore Ridgely of Dover successfully undertook the management of several farms. In the inventory of Mrs. Ann Vaughan of Sussex County are farming implements, the contents of a country store, and iron fragments from a forge or bloomery business.

Thus, evidence is present at the end of the eighteenth century in Delaware that women, in a small way, were beginning to assert themselves and take a more active role in society. Such bold spirits as James Tilton and Thomas Dilworth thought that the change was all for the better.

The social structure in Delaware of the 1780s was relatively fluid. Some people, like John Dickinson and the Ridgelys, inherited lands and possessions, which immediately placed them in the upper class. But most of the inhabitants of the state, as elsewhere in the new nation, were farmers of varying degrees of prosperity. A few people were physicians, lawyers, owners of flour mills, and craftsmen in towns.

Below the middle class, poor whites, free blacks, and slaves lived in a very simple and plain manner in cabins of one or two rooms with a loft, often in bad repair. Their possessions were so few, and often old and worn-out hand-me-downs, that appraisers at the time of death of one of them did not bother to list them, as they would bring nothing at sale.

The papers of the Levy Court of New Castle County reveal some of the problems that the poor, the homeless, the elderly, and ill encountered. A mulatto foundling was discovered on the Great Road to Wilmington in 1788. Efforts to locate the mother were unsuccessful. William Tussey was paid eleven shillings and threepence for the nursing, clothing, and burial of the infant.

Elizabeth Dunn had arrived from Dublin, Ireland, in 1774. At first she served a master in Queen Anne's County, Maryland. Later she married a soldier of the Delaware Regiment, but he died. Subsequently she was employed by Abraham Dushane of Red Lion Hundred, but then, in 1788, ill with ague and a sore leg, she could work no longer and sought aid from the members of the Levy Court. She was granted a small yearly allowance. In the same year another elderly woman, Mary Louder, who had taught school in her younger days in New Castle and in Red Lion, was granted relief.

The account book of the treasurer of New Castle County is filled with entries of small sums given to such people. Christiana Hundred responded to the needs of these people in 1785 by building a poorhouse. A few years later New Castle County opened a poorhouse, and soon Kent and Sussex counties followed suit.

Only recently has a thorough study of housing in the state at the end of the eighteenth century been conducted, using computers to aid in the production of statistics relating to building form, size, material, and condition. Probate inventories listing the possessions of deceased persons have been of great assistance. Using such tools, Dr. Bernard Herman has concluded that in Sussex County houses were small (eighty-five percent contained less than 450 square feet), surrounded by a few outbuildings such as a kitchen, smokehouse and barn or corn crib and packed with an average of six chairs, two chests, two tables, three beds, a cupboard, a loom, and a spinning wheel.

In a recent article Dr. Herman presented an interesting picture of living conditions in Sussex County two hundred years ago:

Two centuries ago Sussex Countains were not particularly concerned with the seashore. Of more interest to these early settlers were the marsh hay meadows along tidal creeks and the great timber resources contained in the Burnt Swamp. Agriculture for much of the county was an unpromising pursuit requiring intensive labor for few rewards. In some hundreds, such as Broad Creek, over fifty percent of the land was still in timber as late as 1850. Where land was cleared and improved it was enclosed with post-and-rail or worm fence and the fields within the enclosure tilled by hand or with oxen pulling wooden plows and harrows. Most farmers tilled their land on a three or four field rotation setting aside two fields for corn, one for wheat or some other grain, and one for pasture. Close to the house were peach and apple orchards and a fenced household garden furnished with bee gums. The only notable crop was flax cultivated for the home manufacture of linen. Situated away from the house was an "outfield"—a small fenced plot of land set aside for hard usage and occasionally for a resident tenant's steading.

There were typically few buildings on these early Sussex County farms. The average number of four included the house, a separate kitchen, smoke or meat house, and a corn house or barn all of which were grouped into a line or open courtyard. Over three quarters of all farm dwellings in the early 1800s contained less than 400 square feet of living space under one roof. These dwellings (often listed in court records as mansion houses) were packed with an average of three beds, two blanket chests, six chairs, two tables, two spinning wheels, loom, corner cupboard, and seven inhabitants. Outside the house the same number of pigs as people ran loose in the woods. A cow for milk, sheep for wool, oxen for heavy work and plowing, and geese for meat and feathers added to the general confusion around the house. With few outbuildings in use, tools, farm vehicles, and household debris tended to be left out in the winter.

Dr. Herman's studies based on assessment records have changed our concept of how people lived in the late eighteenth century in Sussex County—and elsewhere in the state. The average family of seven lived in a small one-room dwelling with a loft, crowded with beds and furniture. Sometimes there was a lean-to for a kitchen and occasionally the house was expanded by building sleeping space on the second floor. If so, the downstairs was used like a medieval "hall." Such houses were occupied by persons of all classes and should not be regarded as hovels. They might contain a paneled hearth, fine furniture, and walls filled with soft brick as insulation. While as many as nineteen outbuildings have been counted in inventories, usually there were about three: a kitchen, a smokehouse, and a corn house. Some of these one-room dwellings might be defined in inventories as a "mansion house," since it was the chief residence of the landed proprietor.

In spite of the forests, the inhabitants of Sussex County were not as isolated as we once thought, and engaged in much trade with the outside world. From sheep came wool, which could be spun and woven into cloth for sale. From the forests came wood to be manufactured into planks, barrel staves, and shingles to be shipped to urban areas. Inventories of stores reveal the great array of British hardware, textiles, and spices for sale. Observations of Thomas Robinson on the eve of the Revolution reveal that there was more corn along with a little wheat shipped out of streams in Sussex County than formerly believed.

Study of the assessment list of 1797 in Kent County by Laura Gehringer provided interesting material. The number of persons assessed totaled 3,175, including 562 tenants. The average number of acres assessed was about 100. Of the 1095 houses assessed there were 370 log, 276 frame, and 106 brick. Most of the brick houses were located in Duck Creek Hundred. The number of assessed slave owners varied from ten to sixteen percent of the population, with Little Creek Hundred containing the smallest number and Duck Creek Hundred the largest number. Only twenty-three free blacks owned land. Ownership of cattle per assessed person varied from sixteen in Murderkill Hundred to five in Duck Creek Hundred; ownership of pigs per person varied from eleven in Murderkill Hundred to four in Duck Creek Hundred. Ownership of silverplate was concentrated in Murderkill Hundred with 3,443 ounces and in Duck Creek Hundred with 1,079 ounces. From this study comes a picture of Kent County as an area of small farms with mainly log or frame houses.

A study of Kent County at the end of the eighteenth century by Madeline Dunn Hite, of the Bureau of Museums of the Delaware Division of Historical and Cultural Affairs, supplies additional information. While most of the residents were engaged in farming, others were listed in assessment records and legal documents as bricklayers, brickmasters, carpenters, carriagemakers, cordwainers, coopers, fence viewers, hatters, house painters, joiners, judges, lawyers, merchants, millers, physicians, saddlers, sawyers, shallopmen, shaymakers, surveyors, tanners, tavernkeepers, tax assessors,

weavers, and wheelwrights. Many farmers and tenants supplemented their income by working part-time at these
occupations.

Many residents were victimized by the poor economic
conditions of the 1780s, as evidenced by petitions to the
legislature for the issuing of more paper money or extending
the time for the payment of mortgages. Only about fifty
percent of the county's assessed population were landowners.
While the bulk of the landowners were men, women owned 9
percent of the land, and free blacks about 1.5 percent. By
1797 approximately eighteen percent of the county's assessed
population were tenants. The largest number of assessed
tenants (313) lived in Duck Creek Hundred, and the fewest
number (11) in Mispillion Hundred.

The Hite study found that the unfavorable economic conditions of the 1780s were reflected in Orphans Court records,
which frequently describe both the houses of tenants and
landowners as being in "midling repair," "ruinous condition," "out of repair," or "tolerable repair." Poor economic
conditions resulted in the imprisonment of men for nonpay-
ment of debts, seeking welfare aid from the Levy Court,
asking for admission to the county poorhouse in the late
1790s, or indenturing children at a tender age.

While bad times continued for some elements of the population in the 1790s, for others life improved. A variety of
businesses was established in this decade such as tanyards,
grain stores, mill seats, blacksmith shops, taverns, fulling
mills, warehouses, storehouses, wheelwright shops, barkhouses,
weaving shops, currying shops and saw mills. The larger
number of businesses (eighty-four) appeared in Murderkill
Hundred followed by Duck Creek Hundred with sixty-four.

In the 1790s the population increased. The number of free
persons grew from 16,620 in 1790 to 18,009 in 1800, while
the number of slaves decreased from 2,300 to 1,485. Because
of this growth, such communities as Camden, Milford, and
Frederica emerged as villages, while Duck Creek and Dover
increased in population. Local merchants imported more goods

from urban areas and Wilmington newspapers circulated throughout the county.

Throughout this twenty-year period Kent County witnessed many changes. Its agricultural activities survived droughts, insect infestations, and inflation. Many slaves became freedmen. Construction activities flourished, especially in the 1790s. The State House was completed by 1792, domestic dwellings and outbuildings were repaired or constructed, and building materials such as glass were often imported from Philadelphia. Eastern Shore craftsmen found employment in the county. Certainly the Kent County of 1800 was different from that of 1780. Studies of a similar nature of the other two counties would probably reveal an equal number or even a greater number of changes.

Inventories present a detailed picture of how farmers lived in the 1780s. The possessions of Robert Wallace in Sussex County in 1781 were valued at £290 at the time of his death. In his house were seven beds and accompanying furniture, Windsor chairs, and chests. He owned horses, oxen, cows, and hogs, and he grew wheat, corn, flax, oats, and rye. His inventory included two hundred pounds of tobacco, bee hives, and twenty-nine gallons of brandy. In addition to the usual farming implements, he also owned sets of tools used by joiners, turners, and shoemakers.

The possessions of Arthur Cade, probably a tenant farmer, who died in Sussex County in 1784, were more modest. The furniture of his home consisted of one bed and accompanying furniture, two "setting" chairs, earthenware, one frying pan and one small iron pot. These were probably the contents of a one-room structure. Farm animals included one cow, one calf, one sow, and several pigs. His inventory was valued at forty-four pounds.

Arthur Cavender of Sussex County was not any better off and probably lived in a one-room dwelling. Furnishings were what one might expect to find in a residence of a laborer. The inventory was valued at forty-five pounds, including a horse worth fifteen pounds. His belongings consisted of one bed, two setting chairs, one frying pan, one small iron pot, and a case for holding tableware. Livestock consisted of one cow, one calf, and a sow with several pigs. His only farming implements were a plow and a hoe.

Even more poorly furnished was the home of James Cannon of Sussex County, probably an agricultural laborer, who owned one old bed, one old "chear," a prayer book, earthenware, and wearing apparel. No farm animals were listed in the inventory, which was valued at twelve pounds.

In contrast, a small portion of the population enjoyed a much higher standard of living, spending their days in large brick houses attended by slaves or indentured servants and surrounded by fine furniture, books, and pictures. They sent their children to private schools, frequently visited and made purchases in Philadelphia, and participated in numerous social functions with their friends. They had acquired the means to do so by inheritance, maritime trade, milling flour, keeping a general store, raising wheat or operating a forge. Examples in New Castle County would include Dr. John McKinly, a physician and a politician who served as the first president of the Delaware State in 1777 and lived in a large brick mansion on Market Street in Wilmington, or George Read, a lawyer and a prominent politician who resided in New Castle. Examples in Kent County would include Dr. Charles Ridgely, a landowner and a political leader who lived in a large brick house facing the Courthouse Square (Dover Green today); Thomas Collins, a wealthy landowner whose home was an imposing brick mansion at the edge of Duck Creek Cross Roads; and John Dickinson, who owned a brick residence in Jones' Neck near Dover in the midst of several thousand acres of land, but who mainly lived in a brick mansion in Wilmington in the 1790s. General John Dagworthy lived in baronial splendor in the forest in southern Sussex County.

An analysis of the inventories of some of these privileged persons presents an idea of their styles of life. Dr. Ridgely had moved from a nearby farm into the center of Dover near the courthouse and purchased the residence of Thomas Parke, a prosperous merchant. The seven rooms were crowded with the physician's family of five children and their household possessions. Each of the three upstairs rooms contained two or three beds, while three cribs were placed in the hallway. The finest room downstairs was the parlor, which was also used as the dining room. In addition to Windsor chairs and small tables, it also contained a dining table and matching chairs of cherry wood with needlepoint seats. Oil paintings of Dr. Ridgely's mother and first wife decorated the walls. In back of the residence a coachhouse sheltered a phaeton, a sulky, and a cart. To help maintain the house and operate his nearby plantation named Eden Hill Farm, Dr. Ridgely owned fourteen slaves ranging in age from seven to fifty.

Some other Delawareans lived in as fine a style as did the Ridgely family. In the home of Vincent Loockerman of Kent County the patterns of the bed-curtains matched those at the windows. His cellar was stocked with rum, gin, and cherry "bounce." The owner carried a gold-headed cane and a gold watch. The furnishings of the home of another Kent Countian, Thomas Collins of Duck Creek Hundred, included walnut chairs with claw feet and leather bottoms, chairs with damask seats, a mahogany dressing table, and ivory handled knives and forks. In Sussex County the residence of General Dagworthy contained a card table, a backgammon table, and a "spinitt." On special occasions he wore a sword with a silver-washed handle.

At the time of his death in 1784 Caesar Rodney was living in a small house, but it was elegantly furnished. Downstairs was a parlor, kitchen, and passageway, and upstairs was a bedchamber. Among his possessions were a mahogany bed and dressing table, one set of eight chairs with damask seats and another with hair bottoms, several armchairs and an eight-day clock. In the downstairs parlor were four Venetian crimson window curtains and a set of andirons with brass-fluted pillars. Many pieces of silver were listed, including a coffeepot (now in the Historical Society of Delaware) and a teapot. The first item of the inventory was an oil painting of

Queen Charlotte, wife of George III. One wonders if it was the companion picture to the portrait of George III burned in a fire on Dover Green in June, 1776. Rodney's wearing apparel was valued at fifteen pounds, a very large sum for that period. In addition he also owned silver shoe and knee buckles and a pair of gold sleeve buttons. He was the owner of fifteen slaves, whose gradual manumission he had arranged for in his will.

Attire in the 1780s could be very elegant and colorful. Upon great social occasions men of wealth wore brocaded or velvet jackets with lace at the sleeves, powdered their hair, and carried swords with silver-washed handles. Their shoes might be decorated with silver buckles or buckles with gems. Ladies matched this elegance with lovely gowns of damask or silk with full skirts and with "stuff" (cloth) shoes to match. In their hair they wore plumes and ribbons.

The very poor sometimes wore clothing so old and worn that even its color was hard to distinguish. When Thomas Dazey, a poor farmer of Sussex County, died in 1777, his wearing apparel was valued at 1.3 pounds and consisted only of items before which was prefaced the word "oald," whether it be his two "shurts," one jacket, "wone pair shouse," one hat, or a pair of "trowsers."

But members of the lower and middle class often dressed in colorful garments. When James Chambers of Sussex County, probably a shoemaker, died in 1784, his estate only amounted to thirty-five pounds, including a horse valued at ten pounds, but his wardrobe was quite elaborate. He could dress up in any one of several white, striped, or checkered shirts, or wear checkered and striped woolen or linen trousers or one of several pairs of breeches. He had a choice of assorted colored stockings, silver knee and stock buckles, and linen or silk handkerchiefs. He carried his money in a "worked pocket book." In brief, he was an elegant dandy!

In 1783, when young Nicholas Ridgely left Dover to study law under the guidance of a member of that profession in Cambridge, Maryland, his mother carefully packed for him a wide variety of clothing: four ruffled shirts, four plain stocks, one sky-blue superfine cloth coat, one pair of black silk breeches, one new bearskin coat, one complete forest cloth suit, six pairs of worsted colored stockings, two pairs of white stockings, three white cambric pocket handkerchiefs, two bandannas, twenty-one pairs of nankeen breeches, two pairs of white dimity breeches, two pairs of white thread stockings, one new drab cloth great coat, one pair of boots, six towels, four pairs of white silk stockings, one pair of new shoes, one mended, one old, and one new hat, and two nightcaps. One might have thought that he had sufficient clothing with him to last for a year or two, but in the next month his mother forwarded ten new shirts, two pairs of Philadelphia-made shoes, one pair of yellow slippers, and his penknife.

Women dressed as elaborately, or perhaps more so, than men. When Esther Craig, a spinster, died in Sussex County in 1787, the inventory of her estate revealed that she owned a wide range of clothing. She had a choice of wearing ten "grounds" (gowns) of calico, purpose worsted, striped cloth or "scipwork" material; red and striped petticoats; four coats and two "clocks" (cloaks); nine aprons made of "toe" (tow linen) or of checkered or white material; any one of eight pairs of stockings, thread, worsted, and woolen; two pairs of "stuff" shoes and one pair of leather; a "guse" (gause) or spotted lawn bed cap; several bonnets; and black silk mittens. Accessories included a fan and two pocketbooks. Almost as elaborate was the attire belonging to Nelly Draper of Sussex County. Her inventory included a hunting saddle and a gold ring.

But colorful attire was not confined to the middle and upper classes. Advertisements for runaway slaves and indentured servants provide proof that all classes dressed in a similar manner, even though the garments might be handed down from a previous owner or the wearer might own no other clothing than what he was wearing. In 1790 an Irish indentured servant in Milford ran away from his master, a tailor, wearing a new suit of fustian cloth, a coat with half lapels, a short vest with two rows of buttons, black shoes with pewter buckles, and white stockings. Along with him he took a new linen shirt, a hat, and blue flannel stockings with white bottoms. In 1789 a Wilmington master advertised for a young female slave who was last seen wearing a linsey short gown, a worsted cross-barred petticoat, a small black worsted bonnet, white yarn stockings, and low-heeled leather shoes. Another runaway slave, Stephen, trained as a blacksmith, took with him a fur hat, a coarse grey coat of foreign manufacture, an old cloth jacket with London drab foreparts and deep blue back parts, a satinet jacket and breeches, nankeen trousers, a new tow shirt and trousers, a fine linen shirt, and shoes with buckles.

All classes of society in Delaware enjoyed many of the same amusements and recreational activities. Thomas Rodney enjoyed hunting, fishing, playing cards, participating in shooting matches, elections, hangings, and horse racing just as his father had done. In a letter he reminisced about social activities in the middle of the century:

> The manners and customs of the white people when I first remember were very simple, plain and social. Very few foreign articles were used in this part of the country for eating, drinking or clothing. Almost every family manufactured their own clothes, and beef, pork, poultry, milk, butter, cheese, wheat and Indian corn were raised by themselves, served them with fruits of the country and wild game for food; and cider, small beer, and peach and apple brandy for drink. The best families in the country but seldom used tea, coffee, chocolate or sugar, for honey was their sweetening. The largest farmers at that time did not sow over twenty acres of wheat, nor tend more than thirty acres of Indian corn, and there was very few of this sort, so that all the families in the country had a great deal of idle time, for the land being fertile supplied them plentifully by a little labor, with all

that was necessary, nay with great abundance, more than enough, grudged nothing to those who happened to want. Indeed, they seemed to live as it were in concord; for they constantly associated together at one house or another in considerable numbers, to play and frolic, at which times the young people would dance, and the elder ones wrestle, run, hop, jump or throw the disc or play at some rustic and manly exercises. On Christmas eve there was a universal firing of guns, and traveling round from house to house during the holiday, and indeed, all winter there was a continual frolic at one house or another, shooting matches, twelfth-cakes, etc.

The amusements that Thomas Rodney mentioned as popular in the middle of the eighteenth century remained so in the 1780s. His own diaries and memoranda are filled with accounts of visiting, attendance at dinners and balls, betting on horse races, watching the courts in session, voting in elections, and frequenting taverns. In 1782 Robert Kirkwood and Joseph Anderson arranged for three days of horse racing near Newark for prizes, and a similar event was conducted at Middletown in 1783. In Delaware newspapers the services of horses, like "Cub," for breeding were advertised and attention paid to their lineage.

The Ridgely family letters of this period reveal a social life in which churchgoing, reading, spontaneous and formal gatherings, dancing, and lengthy visits of several weeks to friends were common. Some of the Ridgely daughters took dancing lessons at school in Maryland, and a manuscript dance book giving directions on how to perform the latest dance steps is included in the records of the family. The Ridgely letters frequently mention the names of friends who drank or gambled too much. On one occasion Mrs. Ann Moore Ridgely warned her sons against "gaming" in any form and com-

o, triple 60.
her from fo-
not to break
office; to be
tter they de-
rs delivered.
any poft or
incorporate.
er letters to
of poftage.
paid for in
exprefs, or
poft-office.
nent of mo-
mail to fuffer
ers of newf-
ther printer
on other

boats; the
not exceed-
ral other lefs

nd Polly, S.
att, T. Men-

6th inft. his
o, Captaia
ville Packet,

via and Can-
nd the brig
Madeira and

fides her o-
nd dollars in

the weather
lly, of New-
on Sandy
alt; the rig-
s, bound to

ia and floop
Captain Ken-
ham that he

Wilmington, March 19, 1790.

The elegant HORSE

CUB,

Will cover this feafon,

At the ftables of the fubfcriber, the fign of the Indian King, Market-ftreet, Wilmington, State of Delaware, for Two Guineas each mare, and Five Shillings to the groom, at the time of covering; or Three Guineas and Five Shillings the 15th of Auguft next. No mare will be received without the terms are complied with. His value as a covering Horfe, for which alone he has always been kept, may be judged of by the great price at which he has been held, and fold. He was bred by Major Thornton, of Virginia, who exchanged him for property of the value of two thoufand fix hundred pounds

CUB's figure is as complete as imagination can form. He is a beautiful bay, full 15 hands and an half high, handfomely marked with a ftar, fnip, and white hind foots and his colts are now abfolutely the firft running horfes on the continent, and not exceeded by any for the faddle.

He was got by Yorick, his dam by Silver Legs, his grand-dam was bred by Colonel Hodgfon, in Yorkfhire, and was got by Cub, fon of Old Fox and the warlike Galloway, her dam by Terefmond, fon of Bolton Stirling and young Cadis's dam, her grand dam by fecond brother to fnip, her great grand-dam by Mogul, brother to Babram, her g g grand-dam by Sweepftakes, fire to the dam of Whiftle-Jacket, her g g g grand-dam by Bay Bolton and fifter to Stover, her g g g g grand-dam by Curwin's bay Barb, her g g g g g grand dam by Curwin's Old Spot, her g g g g g g grand-dam by White-legged Lowther Barb.

Good pafture will be provided for the Mares, at 3f6 per week, and every attention will be paid them; but they muft remain at the rifque of the owners.

quenca to r
ed for payr

Y vi
dire
hou
on Friday
a Plantatic
or Dwellin
erected, fit
to the Boro
by lands of
Crips, and
acres and a
ject to an a
payable to
the borough
cution as th

New-Ga

The fub
Pu

S

In the HO
FUSSEL

Englifh
Arithme
and the
Navigat
Branche
requirec

All poffi
children, a
worthy of

Wilmin

To be
On Wedne
late dw
Redlion

HE
hou
tion
where att

Oysters For Sale At The Sign of The Fox In Frederica

gers for New-Caftle and this Port early in the Spring.

the lan-
ps, each
ers over
phts of
ch is to
is to be
e effects

NOTICE.

The fubfcriber refpectfully informs the public that he has
opened an

twenty
itchen ;

OYSTER HOUSE,

In the village of Frederica,

In the brick houfe where Francis Johnfon formerly
lived;

Where gentlemen and ladies will meet with good enter
tainment. He has engaged Oyfters from Rehoboth Bay
once a month, until they are out of feafon. Gentlemen for
hunter , will be fupplied with every refrefhment after a
chaje at the fign of the Death of the Fox,

By their humble Servant,

Jofeph Dyer.

ie oil is
lve feet
and co-
is to be
g cedar
vo hun-
red by a

Kent County, Nov. 6

he con-
will be
ce will
ference

To the Public.

Delaware Gazette, December 6, 1790.

mented, "Here, you know, Cock fighting, Cards, Billiards,
and Dice playing [are] as common as drinking." When the
Ridgely children visited in Wilmington, they enjoyed walking along the Brandywine, bathing in that stream in the
summertime, visiting the Gilpin papermill, attending dances,
and socializing with friends.

The activities of Mrs. Aletta Clarke, who lived near the
Broadkiln River in Sussex County, are quite in contrast with
those of Mrs. Ridgely. The most obvious thing about her
diaries is the religious intensity of the writer. In addition to
frequent attendance at Sabbath services, revivals, and quarterly meetings, Mrs. Clarke also participated in quilting parties, weddings, and singing school. In the summer she
commented upon activities at the nearby beach, where stands

sold meat, bread, wine, rum, raisins, and cake. At Christmas time the family usually visited her mother and father, but no reference is made to an exchange of presents or special observance. Visitors often stopped by Mrs. Clarke's home, and in turn, the Clarke family often drove to the residences of relatives or friends. Her husband enjoyed hunting, fishing, and oystering.

Children turned to other outlets for amusement. John Hamilton, a Wilmington schoolboy in the 1780s, read geography and travel books, which for him took precedence over flying kites, playing marbles or ball, and shinny sticks. Wilmington bookstores often listed volumes that they thought should or would appeal to children.

Wilmington newspapers did not usually advertise places of entertainment. Occasionally notices would appear about a tavern changing hands, a musical evening, a lecture, or a singing or dancing school, but there was no reference to plays or dramatic entertainments.

Most holidays were not well kept in the 1780s, but there was limited attention to Christmas and to Twelfth Night. The students in John Webster's school in Wilmington barred him from the building because he wished to hold class on Christmas Day in 1786. But an exception came on the Fourth of July, which commemorated American independence. The Society of Cincinnati in Delaware was celebrating that day as early as 1787. The organization was composed of military officers who had served in the American Revolution. The members met in Dover, Duck Creek Cross Roads, or Wilmington. First came a parade to a site or building where a member presented a patriotic address on the sacrifices that his listeners made in the Revolution. This speech was followed by a dinner at a tavern, where thirteen toasts were drunk in honor of the thirteen states in the union. Typical of these were a toast to "the memory of the patriots and heroes who have devoted their lives on the altar of liberty in every age and nation," or to "the glorious Declaration of Independence— May every succeeding anniversary illustrate the wisdom of and magnanimity of that memorable decision."

Celebration of the Fourth of July
by the Society of Cincinnati
in Duck Creek Cross Roads
in 1787

WILMINGTON, JULY 7

Last Wednesday, being the Anniversary of American Independence, the Society of the Cincinnati held their annual meeting at Duck Creek Cross Roads—When they proceeded to the election of officers for the ensuring years: Doctor Tilton was chosen President, Major Patten, Vice-President, Capt. M'Kennan, Sec., Mr. Roach, Treasurer, Dr. Monro, Vice-Treasurer. Messrs. Hazlet and John Adams, eldest sons of Colonel Hazlet and Captain Adams, who fell as victims to British tyranny in the glorious defence of American Independence, were initiated into the society with all the solemnity of that order; upon which occasion several ladies and gentlemen attended as spectators. At dinner Thirteen Patriotic Toasts were drank. The whole business of the meeting was conducted with the greatest harmony and good order. After which the Society adjourned to meet again at New Castle on the 26th day of August next.

Delaware Courant, July 7, 1787 (Microfilm).

The celebration of the Fourth of July in Wilmington in 1791 was especially memorable because it marked the fifteenth year of American independence. The members of the society met on board the *Willing Maid* with Captain Hardin to drink toasts and fire thirteen guns. Then the captain's "barge" used to ferry him ashore, was placed on wheels. With music playing and colors flying, the members proceeded up Market Street to the Brandywine for festivities. On their return to the Christiana River, they were greeted by thirteen guns.

An editorial in the *Delaware Gazette* of July, 1792, expressed what the Fourth of July meant to Delawareans:

Full sixteen years have now elapsed since America was declared free from the galling yoke of Britain's tyranny, and we are now entering on the seventeenth year of that blessed independence, which gave a nation birth, and caused America—oppressed and injured by maternal cruelty and violence by the once beloved mother country—caused America to lift up her head among the independent nations of the world.

The editor concluded the editorial by expressing the opinion that Divine Providence had guided the nation's destiny.

Two poems on the same page contained similar sentiments:

The Anniversary of the Independence of the United States
1792

Let the poets of Europe write odes on the King,
On their musical notes raise so high,
The birthday of freedom we ever will sing,
And rejoice—in the Fourth of July.

No proud, haughty monarch can here bear the sway,
Since tyranny now we defy,
Fair Liberty ushers this joyful glad day.
And proclaims—'tis the Fourth of July.

May Columbians united, preserve and protect
The blessings on which they rely.
Nor with shameful indifference ever neglect,
To remember—The Fourth of July.

This day, be it sacred to freedom and peace,
Festivity, friendship and joy;
May our land in prosperity ever increase,
And be blessed—On the Fourth of July.

Independence

"Hail! Independence, Hail!"
On fate's propietous gale,
Thy various blessings waft from pole to pole;
Till the race of man, adopt one plan,
PEACE, LIBERTY and SAFETY to the WHOLE.

"Hail! Independence, Hail!"
"The Knights of Man" prevail,
Before thy beams the powers of darkness fail,
Earth shall myriads see, ALL INDEPENDENT, FREE,
And TRUTH'S resplendent Glories wrap the ball.

John Parke of Dover, who claimed to be the first Delawarean who enlisted in the Continental Army, published a book of verses in 1786 filled with many patriotic poems and references to Delawareans. In 1789 he published an "Ode" in honor of the Fourth of July in the *Delaware Gazette*. His poem, which is filled with classical allusions and references to Colonel John Haslet, who was killed in the Battle of Princeton, and to other Delaware officers in the Continental Army, is printed in the appendix, along with Thomas Rodney's account of a boisterous Fourth of July celebration in Dover in 1793.

Some people thought that recreational activities held in connection with fairs and public marts contributed to immorality and idleness. They petitioned the legislature to forbid such gatherings. The General Assembly passed such an act in 1786, providing that the organizers of fairs and public marts and persons who sold goods there should be fined and/or jailed. The preamble of the act explained the reason for it being passed: "Whereas it has been too much the practice in some parts of this state for people to assemble themselves together under the various pretenses of horseracing, footracing, shooting-matches, &c., &c., which are frequently made with the intent to vend and sell strong liquors, thereby

promoting idleness, vice and immorality, to the great prejudice of religion, virtue and industry.'' Efforts to have it
repealed by those who opposed the act were unsuccessful. In
1795 the General Assembly also imposed heavy fines for
fishing, fowling, hunting, and attending horse races on the
Sabbath.

Delawareans in the 1780s were not much different from
ourselves. We understand well their goals, such as the desire
to own comfortable homes, earn decent livings, and provide
opportunities for their children. For spiritual guidance they
turned to churches. Having assisted in defeating Great Britain, commonly considered to be the strongest nation in the
world, Delawareans faced the future with confidence. These
were the people who lived in Delaware two hundred years
ago. One wonders whether people living in Delaware two
hundred years from now will continue to share the same
interests.

III ——————————— AGRICULTURE

Most of the population of Delaware was engaged in agriculture, directly or indirectly, as was true of the inhabitants of other states at the end of the eighteenth century. Some persons in Delaware owned several plantations, others one farm, and many more were landless tenants, laborers, or slaves.

Contemporaries often romanticized the life of the farmer. In 1779 a stanza in a poem entitled, "The Farmer," in a Wilmington almanac proclaimed:

Oh happy he! Happiest of mortal men,
Who far removed from slavery as from pride,
Fears no man's frown, nor cringing waits to catch
The gracious Nothing of a great man's nod.

Thomas Rodney, brother of a signer of the Declaration of Independence and manager of Caesar Rodney's farms, loved and idealized rural life. It was appropriate that in 1783 John Parke of Dover, at one time a neighbor of Colonel Rodney, dedicated a poem to him entitled "The Praises of a Country Life," which was included in a book of verses he published in Philadelphia. But few ever attained the happy condition alluded to in the poem. Later, Thomas Rodney became involved with the settlement of his brother's estate and spent time in the "Bastille," the Dover jail.

The frustrations and aspirations of many farmers were

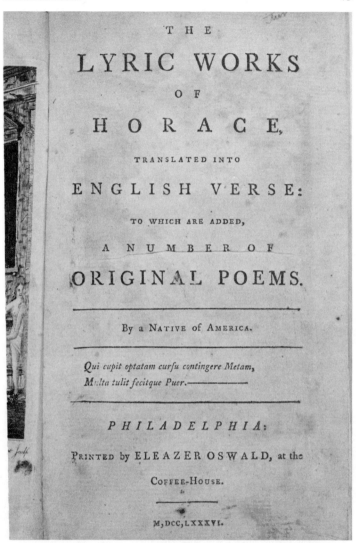

THE

LYRIC WORKS

O F

H O R A C E,

TRANSLATED INTO

ENGLISH VERSE:

TO WHICH ARE ADDED,

A N U M B E R O F

ORIGINAL POEMS.

By a NATIVE of AMERICA.

Qui cupit optatam curſu contingere Metam,
Multa tulit fecitque Puer.————

PHILADELPHIA:

PRINTED by ELEAZER OSWALD, at the

COFFEE-HOUSE.

M,DCC,LXXXVI.

John Parke, *The lyric Works of Horace.* Philadelphia (1786).

EPODE II. THE PRAISES *of a* COUNTRY LIFE.

Addressed to the Honorable Colonel **THOMAS RODNEY,**
Esquire, Member of Congress for the Delaware State.
&c. Poplar Grove, near Dover.

HOW blest the man, who free from care,
(As the first happy mortals were)
Who leads a peaceful rustic life,
Clear of all debt, and void of strife;
Who ploughs with cattle all his own
His small paternal fields of corn!
The roaring seas and din of arms,
Ne'er fill his breast with dread alarms:
He flies the great where slaves resort,
And execrates the jangling court.
The clasping vine, with curling heads,
He to the lofty poplar weds;
Or with his pruning knife disjoins
The fruitless branches from his vines,
And as the older still decays,
Engraffs a founder in its place.
  Along the vale beneath, he views
His wand'ring herds and lowing cows,
Or into jars secure he pours
His virgin honey's golden stores.
Sometimes a sickly lamb that bears
A pond'rous fleece, he kindly shears;
Or when the year begins to wane,
And mellow autumn glads the plain,
Well-pleas'd the rip'ned pear he culls,
The purple grape, rich-clust'ring pulls,
With which, *Priapus* he rewards
And good *Sylvanus* too, who guards
His lines and fences, well repays,
And at each fane his off'ring lays.
Now stretch'd beneath an ancient shade,
Now on the matted verdure laid,
While down the mountain's steepy sides,
The rip'ling stream serpentine glides;
The birds around him freely rove,
Or plaintive carrol through the grove,
And as the riv'let murm'ring flows,
He sinks in placid sweet repose.
  Soon as the rain and snows draw near,
And wint'ry *Jove* loud rules the year,
With hounds the raging boar besets,
And drives him foaming to his nets;

Or spreads his gin around each bush
To hamper the voracious thrush:
The foreign crane, nor fearful hare
Escape the secret tang'ling snare.

But ere a month pass'd fleeting by,
He loan'd it out again on usury.

Arundel, February 24, 1783.

From John Parke, *The Lyric Works of Horace* (1786), 154–155.

Farms for Sale in New Castle and Kent counties
Delaware and Eastern Shore Advertiser, January 10, 1795.

MATTHEW PEARCE.
Newcastle, July 9, 1794.

TO BE SOLD,

The House and Lot,

SITUATE on the Hill, near the Meeting-house, now occupied by John Cummings. The House is a good Story Brick Building, with two Rooms on a Floor, good Garret, Kitchen, and Wash-House, in which is a Well of excellent Water; also, a FRAME CARRIAGE-HOUSE, WOOD-HOUSE, and GRANARY. The Lot comprehends nearly all the Square; part of it is a good GARDEN, the Residue is divided into two GRASS LOTS, on one of which is an old Stable, and on the other an Apple-Orchard and a number of Fruit-Trees.

A large and beautifully situated LOT, called,

The Grove Lot,

Situate to the Eastward and Southward of the Academy; containing two hundred and eighty feet on King and French-streets, and two hundred and twenty feet on King-street; now under Fence, and in the Tenure of Jesse Harris.

Also, one equal Fourth-Part of and in a Brick

Store - House, Wharf, and Lot of Ground,

On CHRISTIANA-CREEK, being the next below M'Comb & Tilton's Wharf.

For terms apply, by letter or otherwise, to the Subscriber, in Philadelphia.

JOSHUA GILPIN.

TO BE LET,

And entered on the Twenty-Fifth of March next,

A PLANTATION, *containing Two Hundred Acres of Land and Marsh; situated in Newcastle Hundred, about one mile and an half distant from the town of New-*

SAMUEL HARVEY HOWARD,
Reg. Cou. Can.

TO BE RENTED,

For a term of Years, commencing on the 25th day of March next,

A GOOD grain and grazing Farm, fituate in Redlion hundred. There will beabout 80 acres of upland, and about 150 acres of good marfh meadow, with a large wood range; fome part of the marfh is already in good Timothy, and it is expected that near three-fourths of it will be fown in September. The foil of the upland is fertile and well adapted either to grain or grafs, and the marfh is inferior to none on the Delaware. The fituation of the buildings is elevated and pleafant, with an extenfive view of the river; the water is very good; and, from the experience of thofe who have refided there, ficknefs need not be apprehended.

Alfo, another Farm, fituate on the river, about a mile below the above defcribed, altogether adapted to grazing; containing about 50 acres of upland, with a wood range, and about 400 acres of marfh, which has always been confidered as well as the upland, of a very fuperior quality.

☞ Thofe two Farms will be leafed on very advantageous terms, and poffeffion may be had of the latter at any time.

MATTHEW PEARCE.

Newcaftle, July 9, 1794.

JAMES GILLIS,
Hatter,

reflected in the names of tracts of land. In New Castle County they included such names as New Work, Jones Venture, Good "Venter," Long Acre, Timber Tall, New Land, Glasgow, Rich Neck, and Warm Land. In Kent County, tracts bore such names as Hazzard's Fortune, Bethel, Rejected Valley, Neglect, Mother's Gift, Turkey Next, James's Addition, Flat Land, Chance, Epraim's Home, Burd's Fortune, Barren Hope, Thomas's Choice, Love Long, Luck, Advantage, and Partnership. In Sussex County, farmers used such names as Puzzle Wit (formerly Advantage), Doctor's Design, Morgan's Delight, Peach Blossom Neck, Dispute, Orphan's Advantage, Koming's Adventure, Good Luck, Fair Play, Heart's Ease, My Delight, Calloway's Adventure, Brotherhood, Newcomb's Barrens, Melson Safety, Nowar Never, Morris's Pleasure, and McGlander's Folly.

Husbandmen of the middle class raised vegetables, fruit, grain, cattle, hogs, and poultry for family use, but they purchased coffee, tea, spices, paper, and hardware at a general store. They used the carpenter's and joiner's tools listed in inventories to assist in building log cabins or frame houses and outbuildings. They were practical people who could cast bullets, prepare apple and peach brandy, and cure meat in "powder casks." By fishing, trapping, lumbering, and working for their neighbors they often supplemented their incomes. Sussex County farmers frequently prepared planks and shingles for sale in Philadelphia. Not much cash changed hands. Store bills of months or years standing were settled by customers bringing in honey, shingles, corn or bacon, or offering their services at harvest time, or for some special work during the year.

Advertisements of large farms for sale or rent in the state reveal that a desirable property included a soundly built house of wood or brick; outbuildings such as a smokehouse, a barn, a granary, and a wood house; a stream of running water or a well; a meadow; a woodland and good soil. Farms located near Wilmington sold for more than those in other parts of the state because of their proximity to markets.

Thomas Rodney presented a view of self-sufficiency of middle- and upper-class farmers in his comments upon life in Kent County at the end of the eighteenth century, cited earlier, but the letters of his brother and farm accounts in general indicate that there was considerable dependency upon other farmers and laborers for help in harvest time and in special tasks such as ditching. Caesar Rodney usually sold his grain in Philadelphia and often had returning shallops bring back items from that city.

In a recent study based upon examination of selected inventories in Kent County at the end of the eighteenth century, Lynn Ellen Peterson attacks the idea that farmers were self-sufficient and concludes that there was much interdependency:

We can no longer be satisfied with portrayals of
eighteenth-century farmers as men of independent means,
as self-contained units dependent only upon themselves.
Evidence suggests that farmers were not seeking a level
of self-sufficiency. Rather, they developed a local economy that all farmers, rich and poor alike were dependent
upon. The poorest farmers depended upon the network
for tools and implements which they could not afford.
Through the exchange of their surpluses (labor) they
could acquire the use of these tools. The middling farmers, although capable, in most instances, of a certain
degree of self-sufficiency, did not achieve it. They might
have owned all the tools and implements necessary to
produce their own food, to clothe themselves and to
perform the tasks necessary in running the farm and
household, yet they were active participants in the local
network of exchange. Middling farmers maintained a
dependence upon it for tools, implements and the majority of manufactured goods such as shoes, carpentry work,
blacksmithing, and like goods. The prosperous farmers
were dependent upon the local economy also; it supplied
them with labor, manufactured goods, and seemingly
tools and implements. Although each of the types required different commodities from the local economy,
each one was dependent upon it.

Her presentation indicates the wide degree of local dependency by different classes of farmers.

Barbara Clark Smith's study of the farming activities of a
prosperous young husbandman in Mill Creek Hundred in
New Castle County indicates that a system of exchange was important in a farmer's livelihood. With his wife and family and
four slaves, Thomas Springer lived on a farm of 129 acres in
the 1790s, raising wheat, corn, rye, and oats as well as well
as fruit and vegetables. He specialized in raising livestock.
Part of the land was unimproved, and another portion of ten

acres was swamp. In any one year about one half of the tillable portion was planted in crops.

His life followed a seasonable pattern. The winter months were a slack time when repairs were undertaken, wood chopped, and fences repaired. That was a good time in which to take care of any legal business and to visit a nearby tavern. The spring was the season for planting oats, flax, and corn. Wheat, barley, and rye planted in the previous fall were harvested in June or July. Meadows were mowed for hay. In the fall came the sowing of next year's crops of wheat and rye. In addition to these tasks other farm duties were undertaken such as the harvesting of apples, shearing sheep, and the preparation of flax for spinning.

While in some ways the Springer household was virtually self-dependent, in other ways it was part of a system of exchange and was increasingly oriented toward Wilmington. Barbara Clark Smith writes:

> The Springers seemed to have found opportunities in many of the changes that threatened other farmers. Thomas could accept the growing power of millers with equanimity because the household was relatively independent of them. The Springers did grow some grain, but they concentrated on raising livestock. The household found several ways to gain from the market: fattening animals, producing butter, selling wool, yarn, and meat. They could live with one foot in a local network of exchange, the other in a wider market. In large part, what made this strategy possible were the inherited advantages that gave Thomas land, livestock, and control of others' labor. He had managed to gain "independence" in the first place only with the help of his successful father, and he prospered only by depending on the work of Elizabeth, some white servants or relatives, and four African-American slaves.

Observers agreed that the best farm land was in New

Castle County, and the poorest in Sussex County, while that of Kent County was mixed. Farmers in New Castle County benefited from good soil, location near markets, and much meadow land on which cattle could graze. Farmers in Sussex County often supplemented their income by preparing planks and shingles in the nearby forests.

At the end of the eighteenth century, farmers in New Castle County began to move inland away from navigable rivers and streams in search of land. Earlier in the century farms might total several hundred acres, but through subdivision among family members and sale, the size of farms were reduced to about one hundred to two hundred acres. Farmers in New Castle County combined the cultivation of grain and the raising of livestock. Wheat remained the principal crop, but sizable amounts of other grains were raised. Most farmers in the county continued their forefathers' system of cultivation without attention to fertilization and crop rotation. LaRochefoucauld, a French traveler, reported in 1800 that "the farms are in general small and ill-cultivated; they receive little or no manure and are in every respect badly managed." Agricultural practices followed an extensive, rather than an intensive, use of land. A large proportion of farm products were sold in market towns like Wilmington, and sometimes they were then distributed outside of the state. Farm property in New Castle County, if located near a navigable stream or near Wilmington, sold for two or three times what it might bring in Sussex County.

From his study of outbuildings on farms, Dr. Bernard Herman believes that as early as 1789 the state was divided into four agricultural regions: the northern dairy region; the central grain region; the south-central mixed farming region; and the southern home manufacturing region. Barns were the commonest and largest outbuildings in the northern hundreds (forty-nine percent), while they ranked third in number in the central hundreds (eighteen percent), and fourth in the southern hundreds (fifteen percent). Corn houses were at the top of the list in the central and southern hundreds. Many farms in the southern hundreds had no outbuildings. A favorite kind of barn in northern Delaware was a two-story structure built on an embankment, with the first floor housing horses and cattle and the second storing hay. The greater frequency of granaries, corn houses, and grain processing buildings in the central region indicates the importance there of raising grain. Small log and frame corn houses in the southern hundreds suggest that less wheat was raised and subsistence farming was common.

The incomes of farmers in Sussex County and New Castle County were contrasted in a study by Jackson Turner Main entitled *The Social Structure of Revolutionary America.* In Sussex County less than one percent of three thousand had incomes estimated at more than fifty pounds, while seventy percent owned property that was valued at less than five pounds. On the other hand, in New Castle County residents owned property valued at two or three times that in Sussex County, and there were many more large farms. Seven percent of the taxpayers reported incomes of fifty pounds or more, while the percentage in Red Lion and St. Georges Hundreds was even higher. The proportion of persons owning substantial farms, with incomes from ten to fifty pounds, was three times as high as in Sussex County. Thus it is evident that the vast majority in Sussex County were farmers and laborers with low incomes, while in New Castle County less than one-third of the inhabitants were ranked in that category.

The best contemporary account of farming was written by Dr. James Tilton in 1788. He reported that wheat was the principal crop in New Castle County, and corn in Sussex, while both of these crops were raised in Kent County. In addition, Delaware farmers also planted barley, buckwheat, and rye. In their gardens were potatoes, cabbages, beans, peas, and berries. Farmers often planted peach and apple trees from whose fruits they could manufacture brandy. Flax provided linen, which could be mixed with wool to produce the fabric "linsey-woolsey." Linen and woolen wheels are

Title Page of a Book on
Husbandry to Improve Farming

THE

PRACTICAL FARMER:

BEING A

NEW AND COMPENDIOUS

System of Husbandry,

ADAPTED TO THE DIFFERENT SOILS AND CLIMATES
OF AMERICA.

CONTAINING THE

MECHANICAL, CHEMICAL AND PHILOSOPHICAL

ELEMENTS

OF

AGRICULTURE.

WITH MANY OTHER USEFUL AND INTERESTING SUBJECTS

By *JOHN SPURRIER,*

AN OLD EXPERIENCED FARMER, LATE OF THE COUNTY OF
HERTS, IN GREAT-BRITAIN: AND NOW OF BRANDYWINE HUN-
DRED, COUNTY OF NEW-CASTLE, AND STATE OF DELAWARE.

WILMINGTON:

PRINTED BY BRYNBERG AND ANDREWS.

M,DCC,XCIII.

Courtesy of the Historical Society of Delaware.

often listed in inventories of household possessions. Bee-hives supplied honey. A few farmers raised tobacco, one inventory including two hundred pounds. Another Sussex County farmer in 1785 had grown four pounds of picked cotton and twelve pounds of cotton in the seed.

The use of fertilizers was not yet common in the state. One observer in 1795 (Scott) believed that not a thousandth part of the cultivated fields had ever been fertilized, even though as many as fifty to eighty successive crops had been raised on the same field. But Tilton, a keen observer, believed that manure was being used more than formerly. Sometimes cattle were penned for ten days in one field, and then in another, in order that the fertility of the soil might be improved. The collection of the Library Company of Wilmington contained several volumes on farming and raising vines.

Wheat and barley, Tilton noted, were trod out by horses following harvest, but crops such as rye, oats, and buckwheat were threshed out by the use of a flail. Two or three horses drew a plow, and four to six oxen were used for this purpose in fallow ground. It took a man one day to cut an acre of wheat with a sickle.

Farmers in Kent and Sussex counties raised cattle, but then found it profitable to drive them northward into New Castle County to be fattened for sale in Wilmington and Philadel-phia markets. Some deeds of New Castle County list the occupation of the owner of a piece of land as "grazier."

Beginning in 1793, Delaware farmers had the opportunity to read agricultural advice given in a volume published by a Wilmington printer. The author was John Spurrier, who had moved from Hertfordshire, England, to Brandywine Hundred. The volume entitled *The Practical Farmer: Being a New and Compendious System of Husbandry* dealt with the raising of grain, fruit trees, and berries, and offered advice. Often British solutions to problems were presented. Many Delaware farmers subscribed to this volume.

According to Tilton, Delaware farms provided ample food for everyone. He mentioned that even the "meanest slave" enjoyed meat and bread every day. Few families breakfasted without a portion of meat. Dinner in the middle of the day included meat, bread, and vegetables. Supper was the lightest meal. Salt pork and back were staple items in the winter and spring, while mutton, beef, poultry, and fish were served in the winter and fall. Almost every farm inventory included several hundred pounds of bacon. Well-to-do inhabitants ate bread made of wheat, while the poor used Indian meal.

To operate farms, labor was needed. Where could one turn? The principal source of labor on Delaware farms is obvious: the members of one's own family. Families were large, and male and female children were expected to aid in chores and in field work. In addition to looking after the house and children, women also worked in gardens, milked cows, and gathered and prepared fruit and vegetables for immediate use and for drying.

Slavery was another source of labor. Inventories indicated that lower middle class families sometimes owned one or two slaves or a black woman and her children. A wealthy person like John Dickinson would own thirty to forty slaves.

Another source was indentured servants, who usually were Scotch-Irish. Their services for a period of years, sufficient to pay for their passage, could be purchased from a ship captain at New Castle. Some of them were trained as carpenters, tailors, blacksmiths, or masons. At the end of several years, usually five to seven, they had paid for their passage by their services and could leave to make their own way in this new land—unless they had already run away. Delaware and Pennsylvania newspapers of the 1780s and 1790s contain numerous advertisements for runaway indentured servants from Delaware masters.

Apprentices were also available to assist with farm work and household duties. Usually they were the children of neighbors. The period of service was usually from five to seven years, and the contracts were terminated when the apprentices became twenty-one. Boys were instructed in farming, and girls in household chores such as cooking, sewing, knitting, and cleaning. Apprentices were admonished in contracts to keep their masters' secrets and to avoid frequenting taverns, tippling houses, or places of bad reputation. They were forbidden to marry. In return for their services, apprentices received food and clothing and sometimes the gift of a new suit of clothing at the time the contract expired. While apprenticeships in the eighteenth century were usually for instruction in farm work or in domestic duties, they were also arranged for boys in cabinetmaking, brick laying, tailoring, shoemaking, and many other crafts. A study of over one hundred apprenticeship contracts in Kent County in the eighteenth century indicates that more than two-thirds involved agreements for farming or domestic duties. Even in New Castle County, where many economic opportunities were available, the majority of indentures for boys were in farming and for girls in household duties.

In addition to these sources of labor, farmers turned to tenants, day laborers, freedmen, and neighbors. With neighbors, some kind of agreement about exchanging services for commodities or labor might be arranged.

The bulk of the people connected with agriculture did not own the land, but came from one of the categories mentioned above. For many of them life was often unhappy and miserable. The working day was from sunrise to sunset, and the rewards of employment skimpy. Even on the Sabbath such duties as looking after livestock had to be performed. Housing was often inadequate and poor. Tenants and laborers found it difficult to secure money with which to pay taxes, as petitions to the General Assembly indicate. Farms were often located in isolated places, as in the forests of Sussex County, and it was a treat to visit the general store in the nearest village or at the crossroads or to attend Methodist services where one could mingle with friends and neighbors and participate in the singing and listen to soul-stirring sermons. Education was limited to a few short terms in a one-room school.

Dr. James Tilton's observations on Delaware farming prac-

tices in the eighteenth century give the reader the impression
that agriculture was prosperous and methods improved, but a
different view was presented by Dr. H. Black in a speech
before the Agricultural Society of New Castle County in
1820, looking to the past. "Our land for the last fifty years
has done little more than starve its proprietors, or driven
them to a sale of it," he commented with some exaggeration.
"The average return on crops for the entire state," he believed, "was five bushels of wheat per acre, ten of corn, and
fifteen of oats, although experiments with fertilizers had
demonstrated the possibility of forty bushels of wheat, eighty
of corn, and two hundred of potatoes." His recommendations
included the abandonment of the four-field system, the use of
fertilizers, and the cultivation of land by the owners rather
than by tenants. He predicted that unless drastic improvements came about, the state would be deserted within a few
years because so many inhabitants were moving westward.
From his study he drew two conclusions: "First, that from
the situation of our land generally in this county at the
present time, when cultivated by the owner according to the
prevailing mode, it nets him clear of taxes, repairs and labor,
nothing. Second, that a very large proportion, indeed, of the
prevailing wretchedness, disease, and distress, as well as the
unhappy degeneracy of morals in society, may be fairly
traced to the poverty of our land as their source."

Delaware was slow to benefit from improvements in agriculture. Not until the 1840s and 1850s was their marked
improvement, first in New Castle County, and later in Kent
and Sussex counties, in part stimulated by the construction of
the Delaware Railroad downstate. Delaware grew in population only one-tenth of one percent from 1810 to 1820 and
only 1.7 percent from 1830 to 1840. In Kent County and also
in Sussex County, there was a decline in population in some
decades after the turn of the century. Western lands were
attractive to Delawareans, and the Brandywine mills could
not compete with flour mills established in the West near the
new sources of supply beyond the Mississippi.

While more than ninety percent of the Delaware population in the 1780s lived in the country, a small number of persons lived in towns and villages. In New Castle County this meant living in Wilmington, New Castle, Christiana Bridge, Newport, or Newark; in Kent County, in Dover or Duck Creek Cross Roads; and in Sussex County, in Lewes. While a few townspeople were lawyers, physicians, judges, or county officials, most were craftsmen such as hatters, tailors, shoemakers, joiners, tanners, carpenters, chaisemakers, or storekeepers. Many residents also owned land on which they could raise food for their families and graze a horse or cow.

Wilmington, with a population of about two thousand, was by far the largest town. Visitors always commented upon its attractive location on a hill overlooking the Christiana and Delaware rivers. French officers in Rochambeau's army on their way to and from Yorktown commented favorably on its many brick houses, straight streets, and markethouse. In December, 1781, one French officer estimated that fifty brick houses had been erected in the town in the previous year. He attributed some of its prosperity to expenditures by French soldiers.

An officer of the Pennsylvania line in 1781 observed, "Wilmington is a fine borough, has a number of regular streets, a courthouse, markethouse and contains about five or six hundred houses . . . with a fine academy on the hill."

Stock of a Wilmington
Hardware Store in 1789

NEW RED & WHITE CLOVER, TIMOTHY & HEMP SEED,

To be fold by J O H N F E R R I S S, at the fign of the *Hand-Saw*, in Market-Street, Wilmington : Likewife a neat and general affortment of Ironmongery, Cutlery, Saddlery, Lintfeed Oil and Painters Colors as ufual, fome of which are as follows, to wit.

THreepenny 4d. 6d. 8d. 10d. 12d. 20d, 24d. and 30d. nails
Smiths Vices and Anvils
London T. Crowley's fteel of a good quality
American Bliftered do. do.
An affortment of flat, half-round, round & 3 fquare rough baftard & fmooth Files
Bench and hand Vices
Iron Pots and Tea-kettles forted
Copper Tea-kettles do.
Frying-Pans and Gridirons

Steelyards from 60 to 250 lb
Temple Spectacles
A large affortment of Brafs Drawer and Defk Handles and Efcutcheon Handles and Rofes do.
Desk, Drawer, Cheft, Book-Cafe, Cupboard, Clock-Cafe, Trunk, Tea Box & Profpect Locks & Hinges
Iron H H L Dovetail, ftrap and Butt Hinges
Brafs Cocks, brafs and Iron Saddle Bag Locks
Long and round brafs tea table catches
Brafs knobs and fcrew rings

Delaware Gazette, February 14, 1789.

Later visitors made similar comments. Jedidiah Morse, in the first edition of his geography in 1789, mentioned that Wilmington is "much the largest and pleasantest town in the state, containing about 400 houses, which are handsomely built upon a gentle ascent of eminence." A few years later another geographer, Joseph Scott, found that Wilmington was "the most considerable and flourishing town in the state."

While New Castle remained the county seat, it had lost out in trade and population to Wilmington. For the most part, visitors in this period considered it to be a town of past importance. An observer in 1784, Joseph Schoepf, found it to be "a little insignificant town" of several churches, a few other seemly buildings, two hundred inhabitants, and "no trade." Morse agreed in his geography in 1789. With only about sixty houses, the town presented "the aspect of decay." But later visitors, such as Scott in 1795 and St. Mery in 1797, predicted that it would again "bloom," when a breakwater for vessels in process of construction was completed.

Their prediction was correct. In 1807 Scott wrote:

Almost all the vessels bound from Philadelphia to foreign ports, stop here and supply themselves with livestock. A great line of packets and stages passed through it from Philadelphia to Baltimore, by way of Frenchtown. Vast quantities of merchandise are sent by this route from Philadelphia to western country. It is at present one of the greatest thoroughfares of travelling in the United States. There are seven large and well accommodated packets, which sail constantly between this port and Philadelphia, and from 10 to 15 heavy waggons, for the transportation of goods and passengers from the peninsula to Frenchtown, besides four land stages.

of New-
a negro
but fays
feet 8 or
r 5 years
tow fhirt,
rfers, old
fays he is
who lives
:lahays, in
of Talbot
requefted
ierwife he

Goaler.

n for any

hels, paid

SCHALL.
y the fub-
Boy, who

3.

E D

he 25th of
rn known

1,

be one of
nd in the
on which

John Moore,

At his Store, the corner of Market and
Queen-ftreets, Wilmington,
Has for Sale,

DRABS
London brown, black, blue bottle, green sa
parlon's grey; fuperfine broad cloths
Snuff, light drab and fcarlet fecond do.
Common do.
Toilinets
Double milled drabs and kerfeys
Twilled Coatings
Duffils & half thicks
Plains & bear skins
Baize & padua ferge
Red, white & yellow flannels
6-4, 8-4 & 9-4 yd rofe blankets
Indian do & coverlids
Serge denim & fagathies
Bafimetts & Shalloons
Lurants & Joan's fpinning
Sitinetts and florentines
Men's & women's worfted hofe
Buckram & wilt boars
Twilled and plain corduroys
Do. velvets
Black, olive, light, buff, blue & claret velvets
Spotted do,
Light, blue & green hair plufhes & tickings
Ruffia fheeting
Apron wide, yd & 3-4 yd cotton checks
Jears, fuftians & fhawls
Chintzes and calicoes
Book & other muflins
Cambricks & lawns
Bandano & other filk handkerchiefs
Large cotton and linen do.
Sattin lutefirings manruas and taffetias
Modes and farienets
Black & green ell wide Perfians
Men's & women's black & other gloves
Pen-knives, razors and fciffars
Knives & forks, fet ftock & knee buckles
Gilt breaft broaches, filver lockets
Fafhionable buttons
Common do.
Throw & twift
Bindings, bobin & garters
Plated Spurs, ivory combs
Plated & other buckles
Men's & women's fhoes
Powder & fhot
Needles & pins
Snuff & indigo
Rum, fugar, tea, coffee, coarfe & fine falt

Contents of a Wilmington Store in 1788
Delaware Gazette, December 20, 1789.

Miscellaneous Wilmington Business Advertisements
Delaware Gazette, January 2, 1790;
Delaware Eastern Shore Advertiser, August 13, 1794.

At the fame time and place will be fold a large BOAT

JUST RECEIVED,

AND to be fold by the Subfcriber, four doors below the Indian King, Market-ftreet, Wilmington, *A Quantity of Good TIMOTHY and* RED CLOVER SEED; Alfo, a very general affortment of Ironmongery, Saddlery, Brafs Ware, Oil, Painters' Colors, &c. &c. on the moft reafonable terms.

SAMUEL BYRNES.

6th Mo. 25, 1794.

JUST COME TO HAND,

And to be fold by the Subfcriber, next Door to the INDIAN KING, Market-ftreet, Wilmington,

A General affortment of *Ironmongery, Cutlery, Saddlery, Brafs Ware*, &c. &c.

JESSE S. ZANE.

Who likewife carries on the Gold and Silverfmith's bufinefs, in all its various branches, and gives the higheft price, in cafh or exchange, for old Silver.

May 30, 1794.

Jofeph White,

At the Sign of the BOY and MORTAR,
Market-ftreet, Wilmington,

HAS juft received a frefh fupply of genuine DRUGS, Medicines, Painters' Colors, Gold Leaf, &c. &c. Alfo, a complete affortment of elegant

LOOKING-GLASSES,

In neat Mahogany Frames, of American Manufacture; which, with the above, he is determined to fell on the loweft terms.

He returns his fincere thanks to his Friends and the Public in general, for their paft, and hopes, by a particular attention to his bufinefs, to increafe their future favors.   June 5, 1794.

Wanted Immediately,

THREE or FOUR APPRENTICES. from 12 to 14

By *WHITE & BYRNES,*
At their Shop, two doors above William
Hemphill's Store, in Wilmington.
12th mo. 19th.

*THE Subscriber respectfully informs
his Customers and the Public in general, that he
carries on, as usual, the TURNING Business at
his shop in Market-street, Wilmington, where the articles in that branch are executed in the neatest and best
manner. All sorts of Windsor and Rush-bottom Chairs,
Settees, Bedsteads, &c. made at the shortest notice --
Likewise SPINNING-WHEELS, made by a complete
Artist, lately arrived from Europe. As the Subscriber
has a large quantity of seasoned stuff by him, he flatters
himself he will be able to give full satisfaction to all
who please to employ him. Orders from the country
will be complied with at the shortest notice, and the work
done on the most reasonable terms.*
Oct. 19.   *SAMPSON BARNET.*

TO BE LET,
And Possession given on the 1st of the 4th mo. next,

December 25.

American Bristles Wanted!

The *Highest Price* given for
American Bristles,
By *WHITE & BYRNES,*
At their Shop, two doors above William
Hemphill's Store, in Wilmington.
12th mo. 19th.

THE Subscriber respectfully informs

Villages of some significance in New Castle County included Christiana Bridge, which was a center for the distribution of grain and flour, receiving grain brought overland from the Head of Elk (Elkton), and, after processing it, shipping flour and cornmeal down the Christiana River. By 1800 it contained several large mills, sixty houses and several taverns. Newport was an important village for the same reason. One traveler estimated that it was about the same size as New Castle, with forty houses, several stores, and a few taverns. Coming from Pennsylvania in 1788, John Penn believed that Newport contained "more houses than Newark and a good brick tavern, which provided proper entertainment for horse and man." Newark, he reported, contained "the most considerable collection of houses I had seen since Lancaster." The village was well-known as the home of the Newark Academy, which had just reopened after being closed during most of the Revolution. Two major roads—one from Dover to Pennsylvania and another from Christiana Bridge to Nottingham—passed through it. Cantwell's Bridge (Odessa) was a center for gathering and distributing grain.

The largest town in Kent County was Dover. Founded by a directive of William Penn in 1683 and laid out in 1717, it had grown slowly. Activities in this county seat were centered in the courthouse square (the green). A block away—in different directions—were the Episcopalian and Presbyterian churches. Farmers found Dover a convenient marketplace, and from nearby Little Creek Landing wheat and provisions could be shipped up the Delaware River to Wilmington or to Philadelphia. Caesar Rodney had once toyed with the founding of a town on St. Jones Creek to be called Rodneysburg, but apparently abandoned the idea because of the shallowness of the water. In 1777 the General Assembly first met in Dover and at a later time decided to make it the state's permanent capital. Legislators held sessions in the old Kent County courthouse and in taverns, but in 1787 a new courthouse was in process of construction, which was to be shared with the General Assembly. In 1789 Dover contained about one hundred houses, principally brick. The four principal streets intersected in the center of the town forming a handsome "parade" (green), where the courthouse was being erected. The principal export of the town was wheat to Philadelphia.

Twelve miles north of Dover, up the King's Highway, was Duck Creek Cross Roads, composed of about sixty houses. Located at the intersection of a road leading from Chesapeake Bay to Delaware Bay, it was an important distributing center for grain from surrounding farms and from the Eastern Shore of Maryland to Wilmington and Philadelphia. Morse thought that the town deserved "a more pompous name" than Duck Creek Cross Roads. About twenty years later the legislature officially changed the name to Smyrna. Historians dispute as to whether the new name was in honor of a grain center in Asia Minor or because of a sermon preached by Francis Asbury. The sermon, based on a letter John, the Evangelist wrote to the ancient Christians in Smyrna, implored the members to be faithful and serve God until death would bestow upon them a Crown of Life. Asbury's sermon led to a number of conversions.

Hamlets and crossroads in Kent County included Fast Landing (Leipsic), so-called because it was the first firm land that vessels came to in sailing up Duck Creek; Johnny Cake Landing on the Murderkill River, later called Frederica; and Mifflin's Cross Roads (Camden), founded by Quakers and located near Dover. Milford was founded under these circumstances: In 1785 Joseph Oliver gained permission from the legislature to build a bridge across the Mispillion River. Two years later Parson Sydenham Thorne constructed a grist mill nearby. Oliver then surveyed and laid out the town of Milford. The name comes from its location at a fording place in the river and near a grist mill. Inhabitants soon began to live on both sides of the river.

A View of the Lighthouse on Cape Henlopen, taken at Sea, August 1780.
Courtesy of the Historical Society of Delaware.

In Sussex County the only town of any size was Lewes. It benefited from its location at the mouth of Delaware Bay, as the headquarters of pilots, and as the county seat. Pleasantly situated on Lewes Creek, it contained about one hundred houses, two churches, a courthouse, and a jail. From the town one could look out upon Delaware Bay, the Atlantic Ocean, and Cape Henlopen lighthouse. However, it was afflicted with "an evil, not much unlike, and almost as severe as the plagues of Egypt," wrote an observer in 1788. "I mean the inconceivable swarms of musketoes and sand-flies, which infest every place and equally interrupt the tranquility of the night and the happiness of the day. Their attacks are intolerable upon man as well as beast. The poor cows and horses, in order to escape from these tormentors, stand whole days in ponds of water with their heads only exposed; and thus, with all their superiority of strength and size, relinquish the pleasures of the pasture through the dread of the insect." Plans had long been afoot to move the county seat into the center of the county, as it took people traveling to Lewes from the southwestern part of the county two days to reach it, but this effort did not succeed until 1791 with the founding of Georgetown.

But Sussex County was changing, and crossroads, fords, wading places, and mills became nuclei around which hamlets were developed. In 1789 Barkley Townsend, the owner of hundreds of acres of land, a shipbuilder, and entrepreneur, laid out the town of Laurel near the "wading place" on Broad Creek. Before 1800 a hamlet on the Broadkiln was known variously as Osborn's Landing, Conwell's Landing, Upper Landing, and Head of the Broadkiln. In 1807 the village was chartered as Milton. Bridgebranch (Bridgeville) had also put down roots before the 1780s. Scott's map of 1795 also included such places as St. Johns (near Greenwood), Dagsbury (Dagsborough), close to the Maryland line in southern Delaware, and Georgetown.

In these hamlets, villages, and towns, farmers often brought country produce in for sale and took the opportunity to shop in stores. Special fairs for the exchange of goods were held twice a year in the principal towns. They were so important for trading purposes that the dates of fairs to be held in Wilmington, Dover, Noxontown (near Middletown), and Newark were listed in almanacs. Some people claimed that fairs fostered fraud and immorality. They petitioned the legislature to abolish fairs. As a result, the General Assembly, as has been noted earlier, passed such an act in 1785.

Towns were important cultural and social centers. There one could seek legal and medical advice, buy merchandise, attend church, visit with one's friends, arrange for an apprenticeship for one's son to a craftsman, and send children to school. In county seats persons could have wills probated, record deeds, obtain marriage and tavern licenses, and attend court.

In Wilmington, services were available that could not be obtained elsewhere. Numerous specialty shops were in business there, and a great variety of merchandise was displayed. Visitors could insert an advertisement in a newspaper, have a handbill printed, and buy books and almanacs. Transportation of passengers or freight by water along the coast or overseas could be arranged, and a stagecoach could be taken to Philadelphia or Baltimore. In the 1780s societies appeared here urging the abolition of slavery and for the purchase of domestic manufactures. Financial contacts might make it possible to borrow money to arrange for a commercial venture in the West Indies or purchase a mill. Part of the funds might come from Philadelphia.

Towns were the yeast in the post-Revolutionary bread and were indispensable in the development of the state. They were important socially, culturally, economically, and politically.

V ——————————— MANUFACTURING

Households in the 1780s manufactured many items. Farmers raised sheep and flax, and their wives carded the wool and prepared flax for spinning and for weaving into cloth. Sometimes cloth was sent out to be sized and dyed, but in a final step it was cut out and made into clothing for family members. Women assisted with butchering and the preservation and drying of fruit, vegetables, and herbs. The male members of the household built log or frame houses and outbuildings, and they manufactured shoes from leather tanned at home. Through apprenticeship or at home, girls learned how to perform household duties, and boys were instructed in the many tasks connected with farming.

Nearby in rural areas were grist mills to grind wheat and corn; saw mills to provide lumber; blacksmith's shops and tanneries. At a crossroads one might secure the services of a cabinetmaker, a clockmaker, a silversmith, a chaise maker, or a carpenter. Shortly after the Revolution, George Crow was a silversmith and clockmaker in Dover, while Robert Ross was a silversmith first in Frederica and then in Milford. Duncan Beard was busy as a silversmith, a gunsmith, and a clockmaker in Appoquinimink Hundred in southern New Castle County. Nearby, at Cantwell's Bridge, John Janvier, Sr., carried on cabinetmaking. In the same community William

Inserted by request.

MECHANIC's SONG.

By Abfalom Aimwell, Efquire.

YE merry *Mechanics* come join in my fong,
And let the brisk chorus come bounding along;
Tho' fome may be poor and fome rich there may be,
Yet all are contented and happy and free.

2.
Ye *Taylors* of ancient and noble renown,
Who clothe all the people in country and town;
Remember that Adam your father and head,
Tho' Lord of the world was a taylor by trade.

3.
Ye *Mafons* who work in ftone, mortar and brick,
And lay the foundations, deep folid and thick;
Tho' hard be your labor, yet lafting your fame,
Both Egypt and China your wonders proclaim.

4.
Ye *Smiths*! who forge tools for all trades here below,
You have nothing to fear, while you fmite and you
blow;
All things you may conquer, fo happy your lot;
If you're careful to ftrike while the iron is hot.

5.
Ye *fhoe-makers*! nobly from ages long paft,
Have defended your rights with awl to the laft;
And Coblers all merry, not only ftop holes,
But work night and day for the good of our fouls.

6.
Ye *Cabinet-makers*! brave workers in wood,
As you work for the ladies, your work muft be good;
And Joiners and Carpenters far off and near,
Stick clofe to your trades and you've nothing to fear.

7.
Ye *Hatters*! who oft with hands not very fair,
Fix hats on a block, for a blockhead to wear;
Tho' charity cover a fin now and then,
You cover the heads and the fins of all men.

8.
Ye *Coach-makers*! muft not by tax be controul'd,
But fhip off your coaches and fetch us home gold;
The roll of your coach made Copernicus reel,
And fancy the world to turn round like a wheel.

9.
Ye *Carders* and Spinners and *Weavers* attend,
And take the advice of poor Richard your friend;
Stick clofe to your looms and your wheels and your
cards,
And you never need fear of the times being hard.

10.
Ye *Printers*! who give us our learning and news,
And impartially print for Turks, Chriftians and Jews,
Let your favorite toaft ever found thro' the ftreets,
The freedom of prefs, and a volume in fheets.

11.
Ye *Coopers*! who rattle with driver and adze,
And lecture each day upon hoops and on heads;
The famous old ballad of love in a tub,
You may fing to the tune of your rub a dub dub.

12
Ye *Ship-builders*! Riggers and *Makers* of fails!
Already the new conftitution prevails!
And foon you fhall fee o'er the proud fwelling tide,
The fhips of Columbia triumphantly ride.

13.
Each *Tradefman* turn out with his tool in his hand,
To cherifh the Arts and keep Peace through the land;

---

rent of twenty fhillings per an

2. a lot of ground adjoining
faid lot, containing about three
ject to a ground rent of thirt
per annum. No. 3. a lot of g
joining Pencader meeting
containing about two acres, fi
ground rent of ten fhillings p
No. 4. a lot of ground, with a
ling houfe &c. thereon erect
on the great road aforefaid, an
ing the Pencader meeting
containing about half an acre
a lot of ground, with a log
houfe &c. thereon erected, adj
before defcribed lot, containing
an acre. No. 6. a lot of grou
a two ftory brick meffuage an
with the appurtenances thereo
adjoining the aforefaid lot,
about half an acre. No. 7.
ground, with a log dwelling
thereon erected, adjoining the
faid, containing about half an
8. a lot of ground, with a go
dwelling houfe and other imp
thereon erected, adjoining
faid lot, containing about h
cre No. 9. a lot of groun
black-fmith s fhop thereon er
joining a lot late of Andrev
which lies between lot No. 8.
lot, containing about one qua
acre. No. 10. a plantation o
land, with a log dwelling hou
ther improvements thereon
bounded by the before defcrit
ground, by the land late of
Thompfon, dec. by the land of
Underwood, and by land late
Thomas, dec. containing by
tion, one hundred and thirte
No. 11. a plantation or tract
with a log meffuage and other
ments thereon erected, bounde
land late of William Black, dec

A POEM PRAISING VARIOUS CRAFTS
Delaware Gazette, February 7, 1789.

Reward of One Penny Offered for
the Return of a Runaway Apprentice

December 2, 1794.

STOP THE RUNAWAY.

RAN-AWAY from the Subfcriber, at Cantwell's Bridge, Newcaftle County, on Thurfday the 30th day of October laft, an Apprentice-lad named JAMES HEATH, by trade a Cabinet-Maker, near 21 years of age: He is about 5 feet 6 or 7 inches hig , pretty ftout made, of a fwarthy complexion; brown hair, (which he generally wears tied or quen'd) but fometimes loofe, when it appears very bufhy and curly; has a remarkable grim looking countenance, and feldom laughs or fmiles; fpeaks low, and has a kind of tremor in his nerves, which may be eafily difcovered, when about any work that requires a fteady hand: had on when he abfented, a blue broad cloth coat, with yellow buttons, almoft new; a roram hat, with a deep crown; a pair of ftriped trowfers; his other clothes unknown. Whoever takes up, and fecures faid Apprentice in any gaol of the United States, fo that his mafter may have him again, fhall receive the reward of One Cent for their trouble, but no other cofts or charges.

A handfome reward would have been offered, but for the following reafon; viz. The term of his apprenticefhip will expire on the 18th day of March next, and he is of a remarkable fullen difpofition, which gives me reafon to think, that if he fhould be brought home, he will elope again, and run me to further trouble and expence; therefore have thought proper to offer fo fmall a reward—but am determined to profecute him to the utmoft, whenever an opportunity offers—as he was very ufeful in my fhop, and the fhort time he had to ftay very valuable to me.

                    JOHN JANVIER, Cabinet-Maker.
Cantwell's-Bridge, December 2, 1794.

N. B. It is fufpected that he is gone to Baltimore, in order to proceed to fea, as he has been heard to exprefs an intention of that kind: therefore, all mafters of veffels, and others, are forbid to harbor or carry him off, at their peril.

JUST RECEIVED,

THOMAS REYN

Rejpectfully returns his thanks to
for their former avours, and in
that he carries on the

Smiths' Bufinefs, at Bra
Mills,

In a more extenfive manner than

He continues to make and repai
raifing millfiones, pa king flour a
for timber wheels, and Fuilers a
prejjes.

Brandt and Stampt in copper
fteel, cut in the neateft manner.

Orders from any part of the co
be thankfully received, and carefu
to.

March 18, 1790.

APPROVED	Suppofed to be LOST bet'
Plaifter of Paris,	George's and Dover,
	The following five DEPREC

Thomas Reynolds, "the Miller's Friend," Advertises His Services as a
Blacksmith. Delaware Gazette, March 20, 1790.

falling back, until he experience the fate of Saratoga—
repeated with 9 cheers.
15. May the greafing of the flag-ftaff be the laft effort
of the enemies of Liberty at Amfterdam.
In return for the compliment paid by the Society to the
Military, they drank the following toaft :
May the Tammany Society continue as they ever have
been firm fupporters of freedom, and the ready defenders
of the laws.
Volunteer from the Chair:
Perpetual union of Sentiment to the Citizens of United
America.

PRICES CURRENT AT BRANDYWINE.

WHEAT, — — 10s. 6d. o 10s. 9d.
INDIAN CORN, - - 4s. 8d. to 4s. 9d.
RYE, — — 6s. 9d. to 6s. 9d.
SUPERFINE FLOUR, 59s. 0d.
COMMON DITTO, 57s.
MIDDLINGS, - - 50s. to 60s.

MARRIED, on Thurfday laft, Mr. Ifaac G. Gilpin,
of this place, to the amiable Mifs Hannah Darlington, of
Birmingham.

DIED, Mrs. Morris, wife of Capt. Morris, of this
place.

onable plated fhoe and knee buckles double and fin-
gle chapes. Metal and plated childrens clafps.
Alfo, per Suip Adriana, Capt. Robinjon, an offortment of
Woollens, flannels, baizes and blanketing,
by the Bale or piece.

Mill Machinery.

ALL perfons concerned in manufacturing grain
into flour, are invited to fee a complete model
of my improvement in that art, which will be fhewn
at my houfe, nearly oppofite the Academy, between
the hours of four and five in the evening during the
next week.
OLIVER EVANS.
Wilmington, Oct. 2, 1790.

Five Pounds Reward.

RAN away from the fubfcriber living
in St. Georges hundred, New-Caftle
county, Delaware ftate, on the 6th of this
inftant, a Negro man named Jonas, about

Grain quotations at Brandywine, *Delaware and Eastern Shore Advertiser*, December 17, 1794.

Oliver Evans Displays Machinery for sale. *Delaware Gazette*, October 2, 1790.

Grist Mills for Sale

necessity of proceeding against them, as
the law directs ; and all those that have
any demands against him are desired to
call upon him.

                        Hezekiah Niles.
Wilmington, October 1, 1789.

FOR SALE,
A good Merchant and Saw Mill,

SITUATE in Christiana hundred,
New-Castle county, Delaware state,
9 miles from Wilmington, 8 from Newport and 1 from the road leading from
Lancaster to Newport, where large quantities of wheat may be purchased ; on an
excellent stream of water, there are two
water wheels, two pair of stones (three
of which are burrs) and three boulting
reels, suitable to carry on business to advantage—Likewise on said premises, a
good stone dwelling house and good
barn. The mill to be sold with or without the farm, as may best suit the purchaser. For terms, apply on the premises, to
Oct. 7.   *John Garrett.*

GRACE MILLIGAN takes this method to inform the public, that
she has been solicited to come to Wil-

[V O L. V.]   W

T O B E L E T,
And may be entered on immediately,

A GRIST MILL, in very good order for grinding merchant work,
distant one mile and a half from Duck-
Creek Cross-Roads, in Kent county, Delaware state, and known by the name of
Griffin's Mill—turned by a neverfailing
stream of water. Likewise a good dwelling house, suitable for a genteel family,
with a small house convenient for a cooper. It is well known that there is not
a better place on the continent for pur-
chasing wheat, and the advantage is great
which arises from the ready sale for the
offal of grinding. Any person or persons inclining to rent, may know the
terms by applying to Mr. Thomas Parke
at said Cross-Roads, or to the subscriber
on the premises.
Oct. 28.   *Samuel Griffin.*

Delaware Gazette, November 4, 1789, November 21, 1789.

To the Millers.

THE Subfcribers have a Merchant-Mill on Redclay Creek, 3 Miles above Newport, Newcaftle County, Delaware, with Evans's new-invented Elevators and Hopperboys erected in her, which does the principal Part of the Work. One of the Elevators receives the Wheat at the Tail of the Waggon, and carries it up into Garners, out of which it runs through Spouts into the Screen and Fan, through which it may be turned as often as neceffary, till fufficiently cleaned; thence into a Garner over the Hopper which feeds the Stones regularly.—Another Elevator receives the Meal when ground and carries it up, and it falls on the Meal-loft, where the Hopperboy receives it and fpreads it abroad thin over the Floor, and turns it over and over perhaps an hundred Times and cools it compleatly, then conveys it into the Boulting-Hopper, which it attends regularly; faid Elevator alfo carries up the Tail Flour with a Portion of Bran, and mixes it with the ground Meal to be boulted over, by which means the Boulting is done to the greateft Perfection poffible, and the Cloths will be kept open by the Bran in the hotteft Weather without Knockers.—All this is done without Labour, with much lefs Wafte, and much better than is poffible to be done by Hand, as the Miller has no need to trample in the Meal, nor any way to handle or move it from the Time it leaves the Waggoner's Bag, until it comes into the fuperfine Cheft ready for Packing.—The whole Expence of the Materials and erecting faid Machinery will not exceed from Twenty to Forty Dollars, as the Mills may differ in Conftruction. One Hand can now do the Work that ufed to employ two or three, two Hands are able to attend a Mill with two Waterwheels and two Pair of Stones fteady running, with very little Affiftance, if the Machinery be well applied—They are fimple and durable, and not fubject to get out of Repair. If Millers will think on this when they are fatigued carrying heavy Bags, or with hoifting their Wheat or Meal, fpreading to cool, and attending the Boulting-Hopper, Screen and Fan, and when they fee the Meal fcattered over the Stairs, &c. wafting, or when they hoift their tail Flour with the Bran to boult over—and when their Flour is fcraped for neglect in Boulting, and when the Superfine is let run into the Middlings by overfeeding, &c, &c. and confider that thefe Machines will effectually remedy all this, and fave great Expence in Wages, Provifions, Brufhes and Candles—and he may conclude that it is not beft to continue in the old Way, while fuch excellent Improvements are extant. Thofe who choofe to adopt them, may have Permiffion, with full Directions for erecting them, by applying to OLIVER EVANS, the Inventor, who has an exclufive Right, or to either of the Subfcribers.   JOHN THEOPHILUS, &
OLIVER EVANS.

N. B. Farmers and others may have Wheat ground during the Winter Seafon at faid Mill (on good Burrs and all Things in the beft Order) with great Care and Difpatch, at the low Rate of Thirty Shillings per 100 Bufhels, or Eighteen Shillings per Load.
Redclay Creek, Dec. 19, 1787.

Lancafter : Printed by STEEMER, ALBRIGHT & LAHN, *a few doors fouth of the Court-Houfe.*

id Elevators will Hoift Water to any Defired Heighth for the Purpofe of Watering Meadow at a very Small Expence Oliver Evans

To the Millers. Broadside, 1787. Courtesy of the Massachusetts Historical Society.

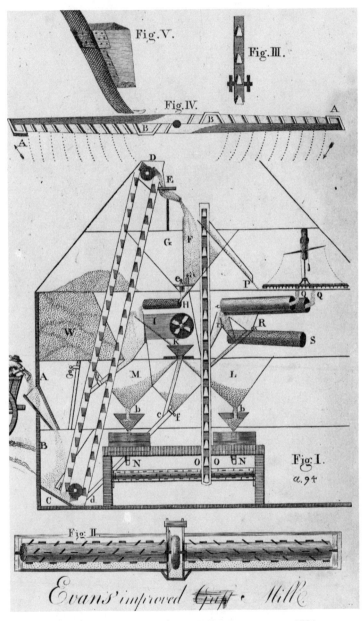

Earliest Illustration of the Evans' Flour Mill Improvements, 1791.
Courtesy of the Hagley Museum and Library.

Advertisements of Two
Cloth Mills

Sept. 25. Henry Pafchall.

NOTICE.

The fubfcribers take this method to inform the public, that they have erected a

FULLING MILL

ON Brandywine, about one quarter of a mile above the bridge, near Wilmington, where the bufinefs in all its various branches of *Fulling*, *Dying* and *Dreffing Cloath* of all kinds ; and likewife, Cotton and linen yarn dyed blue, and other colors, in the beft manner, will be carried on by John Aitkin & Co. Aitkin having wrought in fome of the principal manufactories in Great-Britain, has acquired a perfect knowledge of the bufinefs. He carried it on for fome years in the Great Valley, where he gave general fatisfaction : and in that time he dyed fome pieces for gentlemen in Wilmington, which were allowed to be the beft finifhed of any ever done here. The fituation is very convenient for people coming to Wilmington market or Brandywine mills.

Thofe who pleafe to favor him them with their work may depend on having it done with the greateft care and difpatch.

Fleming & Anderfon.

Wilmington, Sep. 20.

TO BE SOLD.

Public Notice.

THE *fubfcriber living near New-Ark, New-Cafile county, will comb wool, either white, colored or mixed, he will weave cloth & blankets either twilled or plain, he alfo dyes fcarlet, & will clean cloaks or any other wearing apparel of that color and make it as bright, as it was when it came from the fhop, he dyes faxon green and blue. And as he is well acquainted with the dyes above named (which are little known here) and that he has pleafed his employers in the woollen way hitherto, the friends to American manufactures may depend that their commands in this line, will be executed with fidelity, difpatch, and upon the moft reafonable terms, by one who ardently wifhes to promote our home made cloths of every defcription.*

James Popham.

N. B. *Wool or country produce will be taken for pay.*

June 26.

Delaware Gazette, July 10, 1790. September 25, 1790.

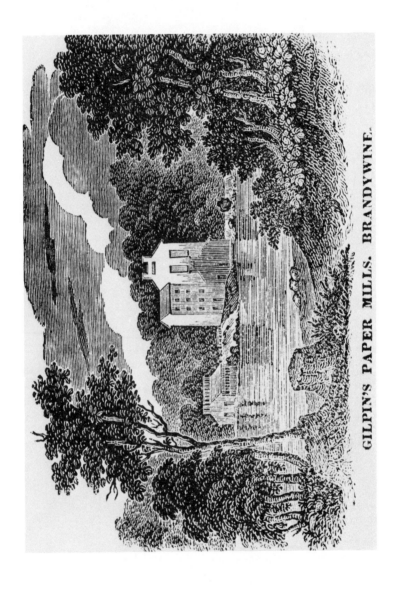

Gilpins' Paper Mills, Brandywine.
Courtesy of the Hagley Museum & Library.

Corbit conducted a chaise and chair-making business. In Lewes, John Orr worked at being a carpenter, a joiner, a shop joiner, and a cabinetmaker. These are just a sample of the products provided by craftsmen in small communities.

More people were employed in manufacturing or the production of items for sale in Wilmington than in any other part of the state. In 1791 a survey found that 552 persons were engaged in manufacturing or working as tradesmen. The twelve merchant mills employed forty-five men. Other persons worked as coopers (fifty-nine), wool and cotton card makers (fifty-five), shoe and boot makers (forty-two), and carpenters (forty-two). Some people found employment in saw mills, paper mills, slitting mills, barley mills, snuff mills, or as watch and clockmakers, makers of spinning wheels and chairs, pump makers, comb makers, or as ship carpenters or boat builders. Altogether, twenty-six occupations were listed, a few in which women and children were employed.

Wilmington had a thriving trade. In 1787 the town exported 22,239 barrels of flour and 5,298 of cornmeal, as well as large quantities of pine boards, staves, and shingles brought up from Sussex County. Imports were mostly rum, sugar, molasses, and coffee. In 1791 exports totaled two hundred thousand dollars.

By far, the most important manufacturing in the state was the production of flour and cornmeal in merchant mills along the Brandywine. The water power of this stream, the location near abundant supplies of grain, the ease of shipment from the Delaware River, and the accumulation of capital from commerce contributed to making the Brandywine area the center of flour production in the United States.

During the Revolution these mills were of so much importance to the Continental Army that George Washington ordered the grindstones concealed when the British approached in September, 1777. Joseph Tatnall was the most important miller, supplying flour for the Continental Army and enjoying a friendship with General Washington, who once visited him in his home. At Tatnall's death in 1813 his estate amounted to more than two hundred thousand dollars.

Every visitor to the Brandywine was impressed with the operation of the mills, especially after machinery invented by Oliver Evans was installed. It was fascinating to see how rapidly wheat was converted into flour, and the ships were loaded. An English traveler in 1786 (Hunter) thought the Brandywine mills "the first in America and perhaps in the world." Dr. James Tilton, a keen observer of Delaware agriculture, mentioned in 1788 that "in Delaware the manufacture of flour is supposed to be in the utmost perfection . . . in [any] like space of ground in the world." The *Delaware Gazette* mentioned that the stream "affords perhaps the best situation for mills in the world." In the fall and winter of 1790 these mills produced fifty thousand barrels of flour and a much smaller quantity of cornmeal from 308 thousand bushels of wheat and corn, an amount equal to the export of these articles from Philadelphia for one year. About two hundred men were connected with the operation of the mills: more than forty as millers, more than fifty as coopers, and the remainder as members of the crews of twelve vessels involved in the transport of grain, flour, and cornmeal.

Much of the grain to keep the Brandywine mills operating came from farms in Kent and Sussex counties. Prior to the Revolution Thomas Robinson once estimated that from ten streams in those two counties 370 thousand bushels of Indian corn, 275 thousand of wheat, and thirteen thousand of oats were shipped annually, as well as barley, flour, and pork. Other sources of grain were farms in southeastern Pennsylvania and on the Eastern Shore of Maryland.

Some of the ships involved in this trade were constructed in Delaware. Records of colonial shipping in the port of Philadelphia show that "snows," sloops, schooners, and shallops were built on almost every stream in Delaware: the Christiana, White Clay, Appoquinimink, Duck Creek, St. Jones, Murderkill, Mispillion, Cedar, and Indian River Inlet as well as at Lewes and along the Nanticoke. As early as

1737, vessels were being constructed on the Broadkiln. From 1760 to 1773, thirteen schooners and one sloop, ranging in size from seven to thirty tons, were registered in Philadelphia as being built on that Delaware stream. Barkley Townsend, the founder of Laurel, was engaged in shipbuilding on the Nanticoke in the 1780s. The names of vessels constructed in the three lower counties before the Revolution read like a poem of men's hopes and dreams: *Happy Return, Speedwell, Defiance, Swan, Charming Polly, Mary, Endeavour, Hawk, Humming Bird, Delaware, Greyhound, Hopewell, Chance, Dolphin, Farmer's Delight, Carpenter's Delight, Neptune,* and *Peace*.

During the Revolution few vessels were built because of the disturbed times, but shipbuilding resumed afterward. The British consul in Philadelphia claimed in 1788 that in the previous five years, six brigantines, one schooner, and three sloops had been constructed in the state. Six vessels called Wilmington their home port, but they were so small that their total tonnage amounted only to 510 tons.

A new enterprise began in Wilmington in 1787 with the establishment of a paper mill on the Brandywine by Joshua and Thomas Gilpin. They were at home in both Wilmington and Philadelphia. A plea for rags soon appeared in the *Delaware Courant,* and a handbill was issued with the same message. From the beginning, women and children were employed in the mill. The British consul of Philadelphia feared American competition in this line so much that in 1788 he forwarded samples of Gilpin paper to England for comparison. These sheets are still preserved in the Public Record Office. Later, in the 1790s, Joshua Gilpin spent several years in the British Isles, observing manufacturing, writing down his observations, and making drawings in his journal. The reports on papermaking he sent to his brother, Thomas, prepared the way for the latter's invention and patent of the first "endless" papermaking machine in America, on the Brandywine in 1817.

Before the Revolution, iron had been extracted from "Iron

Hill'' near Newark and also from the swamps of Sussex
County. Whether forges and furnaces continued to operate in
Sussex County during the Revolution is uncertain. The inven-
tory of Ann Vaughan of Sussex County in 1781 included
"Pigg iron, scraps & half blooms," and other references to
iron manufacturing, as did that of her son Edward, in 1782.
On the assessment lists of Sussex County, in 1784 the Deep
Creek Furnace Company was taxed forty pounds. By 1793 at
least one forge was in operation. Scott's geography published
in 1795 mentioned that forges were operating in Sussex
County "a little," and the accompanying map in the volume
showed the location of Douglass's and Lightfoot's furnaces.
In Wilmington, Richards and Seale manufactured nails in a
slitting mill in 1789, and a similar enterprise was carried on
along the Brandywine by Rumford Dawes.

Lumbering was important in Kent and Sussex counties.
Thomas Robinson estimated on the eve of the Revolution that
more than a million shingles and a million staves were shipped
from those two counties annually. General John Dagworthy,
with his thousands of acres in Sussex County, was clearly the
king of the lumbermen. In his inventory of 1784 were listed
"oak scantling, pine planks sold at mill, cedar plank neat"
valued at 260 pounds. In addition, there were three hundred
thousand shingles ready for shipment in the swamp and more
than twelve thousand at the landing. Altogether, these items
were valued at 1,053 pounds.

Tanneries were in operation in or near many towns in the
state. In 1791 Jacob Broom advertised a tanyard for sale in
Wilmington consisting of a stone bark house, currying shop,
mill house, and slaughterhouse with a capacity for four hundred hides. Another asset was a "never-failing" stream. In
the same year the tannery of Johnson and Wilson in Wilmington was advertised for sale. The property consisted of
eighteen vats, three limes and a water pool, a beam house,
slaughterhouse, and stable. Occasionally advertisements appeared for apprentices in tanning and currying, as for one at
Fast Landing (Leipsic) in Kent County in 1790.

After the Revolution, Delawareans again became dependent upon Great Britain for many items. By 1790, Wilmington stores were filled with British merchandise such as china, cloth, hardware, and drugs. Advertisements announced the arrival of Irish linens and boasted of their quality. Even though there was an association formed in 1788 to encourage domestic manufacturing in the state, many buyers preferred British goods. The inventories of stores in lower Delaware, such as those operated on the Mispillion before 1775 by Levin Crapper and by Daniel Rogers before 1806 and by Ann Vaughan at Vaughan's Furnace before 1781, demonstrate not only the vast assortment of items, but also that much of the merchandise was imported from Great Britain. Not until trade was disrupted with Great Britain before the War of 1812 did the manufacture of textiles and other items in the United States receive encouragement.

VI ——— TRAVEL BY LAND AND SEA

Travelers in the 1780s had a choice to make: to travel by land or by sea and also by what means. The sea was probably safer, except in wintertime. In 1787 the legislature granted to John Fitch a monopoly on the use of steamboats in Delaware waters, and he operated a steamboat on the Delaware River for a short time. A competitor, John Rumsey, asked for a monopoly at a later time, but the General Assembly turned down his request on the grounds that such matters were now controlled by Congress. Steamboats did not come into common use until Robert Fulton perfected the machinery early in the nineteenth century. Before that time passengers and freight for water transportation depended upon a variety of sailing craft.

Roads could be bumpy, hilly, crooked, swampy, and filled with ruts. In the spring they might be surfaced with thick mud, making travel virtually impossible, and in winter they might be covered with mud or snow. Some travelers walked, while others enjoyed the convenience of a chair, sulky, phaeton, or stagecoach.

In her recollections Elizabeth Montgomery of Wilmington presents a charming picture of the means of transportation used by the congregation of Old Swedes Church:

> Many crossed the Delaware from Jersey in boats; others, from the Christiana and the Neck, landed at the Rocks; canoes and batteaux were used, although very

Mr. Fitch's Steam Boat

Columbian Magazine, I (December, 1786), p. 175. Historical Society of Delaware.

unsafe. In winter, rough sleighs, sleds, on runners and jumpers were common, as the snows were deep and lasting. Some went on horseback, with one behind, plunging through the snow. . . .

In summer, an old-fashioned chair with one horse was in use, and once upon a time there was but one of these. A rough wagon would be geared upon Sunday morning for the use of the family; but riders on horseback were most numerous, and many walked. Even in my day, the very air was clouded with dust, and each one had to beware of accidents from the number of equestrians. Family wagons were the next improvement and in later years, phaetons and chariots. Dr. Wharton rode in the former, and Dr. Girelius in the latter; and after a time, numbers of handsome coaches and carriages were seen in the lane.

V LINE.

ball and Newcastle
D-STAGES,

Chambers', at Whitehall, on Mon-
s, and Fridays, for Newcastle ; and
ewcastle, on Tuesdays, Thursdays,
itehall. The Packets from New-
y to proceed to Philadelphia, upon
er-waggons ; and the Packets from
Baltimore, on the Days of the Stages

urn their Thanks to their Friends
eral, and hope they will merit a
friendship.
                    JOHN CROW,
                    JOHN CHAMBERS.

S GILLIS,
Hatter,

ket-street, WILMINGTON,
ts his Friends and the Public, that
le a complete assortment of
en's, and *Childrens' Hats,*
s, and best quality : Also supplies,
the true *A-la-Militaire Hats* for

Militia Companies.

Hats are manufactured under his
best materials, he can with confi-
icle purchased from him, to be the
pes, from his moderate charges and
please, to merit the countenance
d.
ders punctually attended to ; and
ent to wholesale purchasers.
s, 1794.

urt of Chancery,
TE OF MARYLAND,
        JUNE 13, 1794.
THE Complainant prays a Decree
. for recording a deed executed
ne 2d, 1787, by Gilbert Falconer,
c of Kent county, deceased, for
veying unto the complainant in fee,
a piece of ground in Bridge-town,
Kent county, part of a tract of
d called London-bridge, renewed
160l. current money. The bill
ecution of the said deed, the said
fate ; that the Defendants are his
ndant Mary Falconer is a resident
re. It is therefore adjudged and
laimant cause a copy of this order
wspaper of the state of Delaware,
at) in the newspaper of Dunlap &
weeks succesfively, before the first
t to the intent that the said Mary
ans, or any person who may think
l, may have notice to appear in
the first Tuesday in October next,
a decree should not be passed agree-
's prayer.
        Test.
UEL HARVEY HOWARD,
    Reg. Cou. Can.

ph White,
e BOY and MORTAR,
treet, Wilmington,
fresh supply of genuine DRUGS,
ers' Colors, Gold Leaf, &c. &c.
ment of elegant

The Packet - Boat,
HANNAH,
JOHN WALLACE, Commander,
PLIES twice a week between WILMINGTON and
PHILADELPHIA. She leaves the upper wharf,
in Wilmington, on Monday and Friday ; and sets out
from Philadelphia, on her return, on Wednesday and Saturday, in each week. She has hitherto made use of
Chesnut-street wharf, and, in case of change, public no-
tice will be given of it.
This sloop was built in Rhode Island, purposely for a
Packet ; is a strong, good vessel, sails well, and has spa-
cious and comfortable accommodations for passengers ;
having a large, airy cabbin, with twelve births, together
with two private state-rooms for ladies.
Flour, Iron, and Goods of all kinds will be received and
transported to or from Philadelphia, in the above vessel.—
Application may be made to the Captain on board, or to
Wilmington,   M'COMB & TILTON.
July 28, 1794.

PACKETS.
The two fast-failing and well-accommodated
            PACKETS,
    Farmer & Lydia,
RUN from Thomas Mendinhall's wharf, in Wil-
    mington, to the Crooked Billet, in Philadelphia,
on Monday, Wednesday, and Friday, every week, and
leaves the Crooked Billet, on the same days, for Wilmington. For freight and passage, please to apply to
Thomas and Adam Mendinhall, at their store in Wilmington, and to Adam Mendenhall & Co. at their Count-
ing-House, next door below the Crooked Billet, Philadelphia, where any freight for Wilmington, will be received at all times, and no storage charged.
        THOMAS & ADAM MENDENHALL.
Wilmington, May 10. 1794.

Newcastle and Philadelphia Packets.

THE citizens of this State and others, travelling to
    Philadelphia, are respectfully informed, that *The
celebrated Packets,*
MORNING STAR, *Thomas Moore,* Commander :
    And FLY, *Benjamin Jefferies,* Commander,
Alternately leave the Subscriber's wharf, Newcastle, and
Chesnut-street wharf, Philadelphia, every Monday, Wednesday, and Friday morning.—These Packets are built
and constructed purposely for this trade, and have the best
accommodations for passengers. Their cabbins are commo-
dious, airy, neat and convenient ; and by the addition of
folding doors, a part is rendered private for Ladies, or
select parties—And in every respect are considered by the
best judges, the completest, of their tonnage, belonging to
the Union.
To render the passage agreeable, the commanders are
always provided with a supply of the best liquors and provisions, for the refreshment of such as with to be so accommodated.
The Proprietors flatter themselves the reputation these
Packets have acquired, is now well established. The
PRESIDENT of the United States having selected the
MORNING STAR, to convey Him and his Suite from

getown Crofs roads,

om May 1ft to No-
ive Philadelphia on
and Friday, at nine
ad arrive at Chefter-
y, and Saturday, by
ning, to leave Chef-
dnefday and Friday,
noon, and arrive at
Thurfday, and Sa-
toon.
ths of the year, the
every Monday and
the morning, and
Tuefday and Satur-
on. Returning, to
onday and Friday,
rning, and arrive at
d Saturday, by four

arrangement of the
any alteration of the
re before mentioned

*Philadelphia ; David Brinton's, Wilmington ; and at D.
Cook's, Dover ; where the Offices are kept.*
                                    J. JACKSON,
                                    D. COOKE,
July 23.   E. WELSH.

NEW LINE.

The Whitehall and Newcaftle
LAND-STAGES,

START from John Chambers', at Whitehall, on Mon-
days, Wednefdays, and Fridays, for Newcaftle ; and
from John Crow's, Newcaftle, on Tuefdays, Thurfdays,
and Saturdays, for Whitehall. The Packets from New-
caftle are always ready to proceed to Philadelphia, upon
the Arrival of the Stage-waggons; and the Packets from
Whitehall proceed for Baltimore, on the Days of the Stages
arriving.
   The Proprietors return their Thanks to their Friends
and the Public in general, and hope they will merit a
Continuance of their Friendfhip.
   May 21, 1794.   JOHN CROW,
                             JOHN CHAMBERS.

Davis's Golden Tincture,

*A PERFECT remedy for the tooth-ach, fcurvy, and
all fcorbutic humours, from which the tooth-ach may
arife. It cures fwellings in the face, pains in the head,*

alphabetically arranged
II. A table of the c
in dollars and cents.
III. A chronologica
the creation to the pre
            By WILLI
The aftronomical p
                Dr. H
        TO WHICH
The late difcoveries of

The firft American I
                      gr
The firft volume co
two aftronomical plate
   1. Map of the V
   3. Europe, 4. A
   7. Cook's difco
   8. Countries ro
   9. Sweden, De
   10. Seven United
   11. Auftrian, F
   12. Germany,
   13. Seat of war
   14. France divid
   15. Switzerland,
   16. Italy, Sicily
   17. Spain and P
   18. Turkey in I

New-Caftle, Nov. 5.

JUVENIS.

For BELFAST,
The Brig BROTHERS,
James Jefferis, Mafter.
Will fail in all December next.
For Freight or Paffage apply to
                    Vincent, or
                    Edward Gilpin.
Wilmington, Nov. 4, 1789.

For LONDONDERRY,
The Brigantine

MARIA,

*Expected to fail about the 10th of De-
cember next.*
She is a ftrong veffel, and fails well.
For Freight or Paffage apply to
            William Hemphill, or
            Ifaac Hendrickfon.
Wilmington, Oct. 31.

Notice is hereby given,

ftore-
fc-

igh-

on
John

ing-
, and
th by

vinc-

arfh.
d lots,
d and
nferd,

eriff.
2w 92

ionas
on the
, at 2
adts of
ftions,

bo-
houfe,
francy-
r Crips

rove-
Brandy-
olling-

Head of Chefter OB 30.   Abraham Millar.
                              3w 92

For Londonderry,
The beautiful new SHIP,
General Wafhington,
Thomas Forte, Master, Burthen 250 tons,
expected to fail early in December next,
calculated and completely fitted for the
Paffenger Trade, high and roomy between
Decks, and well finifhed. For Freight or
Paffage, apply to the Master on Board,
to William Hemphill, or
                    Ifaac Hendrickfon.
Wilmington, Sept. 4.

THE perfon who has the firft volume of
Rollin's ancient Hiftory,
will much oblige the owner (whofe name is written
to left by returning it immediately.

Maps, such as Scott's, show that the King's Highway began down in Sussex County and ran northward through Milford, Dover, and Duck Creek on to New Castle and Wilmington. From Lewes one could journey southward by way of Dagsborough into Maryland. From Dover the traveler could go westward to reach towns on the Eastern Shore. From Duck Creek Cross Roads, one could journey to Chestertown and to Centreville. Roads from Wilmington led to Elkton and into Pennsylvania. In addition to these main arteries of traffic were branches leading to hamlets and to crossroads. Eventually the so-called roads became nothing but lanes and paths.

The Levy Courts in each county were supposed to look after the roads, and for this purpose overseers of highways were appointed in each hundred. Often inhabitants paid their road tax by working on the highways, but there was no particular standard, and complaints were constant about their condition and the need for improvement.

Petitioners to the legislature from Kent County in 1795 complained that the mode of repairing and maintaining the roads in the county was unjust, ineffectual, and improper, and that they were kept in poor condition. Moreover, the same road tax was paid by a poor man who owed an assessment of one pound as by another assessed at thirty pounds, who owned horses, carts, wagons, and a chaise. The petitioners asked that the road tax bear more heavily on the rich than on the poor.

Petitions to the Court of Quarter Sessions of Kent County in the 1780s and 1790s indicate how important the construction and maintenance of roads were to farmers. One petition mentioned that no thoroughfare existed to a "storehouse" recently opened on the Murderkill River; another asked that a private road leading to a mill be reopened; a third requested the relocation of a road that divided a farm. "Brother Statesmen" (residents of eastern Queen Anne's County in Maryland and of the adjacent forest section of Kent County in Delaware) petitioned for construction of a road from the state line to Grogtown (Kenton) in 1787, in order that farmers might have easy access to Duck Creek Cross Roads. This road would run through several farms, including that belonging to Cheney Clow, Kent County insurrectionist of 1778. Farmers would then be able to market their corn, wheat, and hay more easily and might develop a market for staves and hoop poles.

Travel by road could be hazardous. In 1797 the *American Annual Register* reported that the route from Philadelphia to Baltimore "exhibits for the greater part of the way an aspect of savage desolation. Chasms to the depth of six, eight or ten feet occur at numerous intervals. . . . Coaches are overturned, passengers killed and horses destroyed. In winter sometimes no stage sets out for two weeks." Isaac Weld, another traveler over the same route, mentioned that "the driver frequently had to call to the passengers in the stage to lean out of the carriage, first at one side, then at the other, to prevent it from oversetting in the deep ruts with which the road abounds." While these accounts may be exaggerations, it is true that Delaware was not noted for its good roads. Another traveler in the 1790s, LaRochefoucauld, thought that Delaware was "distinguished by the bad state of the roads." By way of improvement he recommended that the rocks in the roads be broken up into small pieces and used to surface them.

The Ridgely family correspondence contains many comments upon travel. A family friend living in New York believed that to undertake the two-hundred-mile trip to Dover in December 1772 could only be accomplished "at the hazard of my life." On a trip to Newark from Dover in 1794 by Henry M. Ridgely, "the little horse" gave out at Blackbird, and another had to be hired at Middletown. Traveling over a bridge, the carriage broke a spring, which was then temporarily fixed by tying it with the bridle reins. A few years later, in 1798, Ridgely's mother was relieved to hear of his safe arrival in Lancaster, Pennsylvania because of the poor roads and the possibility of stage drivers being "careless, drunken, and ill-behaved."

Travel by road could be dangerous, as noted above. David
Lewis and Lydia Hollingsworth found this out when they
went sleigh riding with another couple. An unknown poet
recorded the sad ending:

VERSES ON DAVID LEWIS AND
LYDIA HOLLINGSWORTH

Give ear ye youth and hark you lovers all,
While I relate a damsel's sad fall,
Who took a ride to see her friends of late,
With her true love who should have been her mate.
Two more of them, young people of renown,
All in a slay did ride out of town.
On their return as they came home again,
The creek was high caused by a sudden rain.
They stopped awhile to see what could be done,
The water deep and swiftly did run.
The slay-man said 'tis dangerous to go through,
You'll lose your lives and your horses, too.
But Lewis drove, the right way did not keep,
He plunged himself and all into the deep.
One damsel caught by one who stood on shore,
The other sunk and could be seen no more.
Lewis fast holding by a bush he caught,
Which from the stream his grand delivery wrought.
But when he found his true love gone,
Run up and down like a distracted one. . . .
To hear him cry, to hear him make his moan,
Would melt a heart, tho' it was made of stone.

(Manuscripts, Box 93, Corbin Papers, HSD).

Alas for the fickleness of men! He was probably the David
Lewis, a Wilmington merchant, who married another in 1794.

Mrs. John Dickinson reported this tragedy to a friend in
1789:

This day week Sally Fisher Corbit was returning home
from ye [Duck Creek] Crossroads, when came to ye hill
at Cantwells Bridge. Ye horse backed till ye carriage
went into the water—by throwing planks into ye water
they saved Sally and her husband with difficulty, her
baby was irrecoverably lost from her arms, they had not
found it when I heard last. . . .

(Mary Dickinson to Debbie Logan, Bureau of Museums,
Dickinson Research Project, File 42/18)

Travel by water could be equally as dangerous. In 1790
Aletta Clarke, a resident of the Broadkiln area (Milton),
wished to visit Philadelphia by shallop, but the voyage took
longer than she had anticipated.

August

27 & 28 We started for Phila., the tides being very low
we could not go out.
29 Still could not get out.
30 The wind being at east we came home.
31 We roade down to the boat again.

September

1   About 1 aClock we got out of the mouth of the
    Creek [Mispillion]. About 4 aClock we struck on the
    hears [shoals], a very dangerous place. The wind
    blew very fresh & the water in a great rage, every
    body on board was frigh'd [frightened], but the Blessed
    Preserver of all poor mortals preserved us through all
    danders [dangers]. Next morning we was up against
    New Castle about 4 aClock. We arrive at Phila. . . .
9   We took leave of our friends and mad sail.
10 We ankor'd about 7 aClock just without the mouth
    of the river.

11 About 2 aClock we found we got on a shole, but it was very calm and smoth. We lay there until flud tide about 10 aClock. We made sail again. Got down against Mushmillion [Mispillion] and there ankor'd. About 2 aClock made sail again.

12 We ankor'd off against Slauter [Slaughter Creek]. The weather very stormy, raining and blew very fresh at East, so that we could not get in the Creek when the tide made. We turned about and run into Mushmillion. There we ashore and tryed to heer [hire] horses, but could not. My two brothers, my cousin and myself, we walked down to Seeder [Cedar] Creek which was 7 mils & there we heer'd horses and got home the same night. Our people was all very glad to see us, being uneasy about us.

According to Aletta Clarke, travel was always an adventure. Her husband was out on a shallop when a "dreadful snow storm" came up. She worried about his welfare and recorded that she was never so glad to see anyone as when he turned up. Once she mentioned that travelers were stranded in three feet of snow on the highway, and she housed them. Her young daughter had the misfortune to fall out of a carriage and to be run over by a wheel, but she was not badly hurt.

Before the Revolution was over, stage lines were again in operation from Philadelphia to Baltimore via Wilmington, as they had been at the commencement of the war. In 1781 a "stage-waggon" with four horses set off twice a week at six o'clock in the morning from Philadelphia, arriving at Captain O'Flinn's in Wilmington for dinner in the middle of the day. Passengers stayed overnight at the Head of the Elk (Elkton), and next day breakfasted at the Susquehanna River, where passengers exchanged places with those coming from Baltimore. The cost of the journey was six and two-thirds "hard dollars" (specie). A similar stage line operated by a different firm opened in 1782. It advertised that passengers would be carried in "new erected stages" on springs, which provided comfortable riding. Gradually the number of stage lines in operation from Wilmington to Philadelphia and from New Castle to the Chesapeake increased. By 1796 a stage line was opened from Wilmington to Dover and Milford.

The people in Delaware often depended upon friends and shallopmen for delivering small packages and letters, as the Ridgely and Rodney correspondence indicates. A postrider had carried mail from Philadelphia to Lewes in 1775, leaving Fountain's tavern at noon on Wednesday and arriving in Lewes at noon on Saturday, a three-day journey. But this service was disrupted by the war.

Congress established post offices. For the year ending October, 1791, the receipts from Wilmington amounted to $159.20, those from Dover to $12.00, and those from Duck Creek Cross Roads to $9.60. By 1797 nine other post offices were in operation at Christiana Bridge, Middletown, Newport, Frederica, Clowes [Broadkiln], Dagsborough, Milford, New Castle, and Cantwell's Bridge.

Accounts by travelers at the end of the eighteenth century demonstrate that travel by land or sea was sometimes difficult. At any time one might face an unpleasant experience. Many improvements occurred in the first quarter of the nineteenth century.

VII ——————————————— EDUCATION

The common schools that most children attended in Delaware—if they attended any in the 1780s—were unchanged from the one described by an Anglican rector in Sussex County in 1728:

> And here is no publick school in all the County, the General Custom being for what they call a Neighbourhood (which lies sometimes 4 or 5 miles distant one part from another) to hire a person for a certain term and sum to teach their children to read and write English for whose accommodation, they meet together at a place agreed upon, cut down a number of trees and build a log house in a few hours as illustrious as that in which Pope Sixtus Quintus was born, whether they send their children every day during the term, for it ought to be observed by way of commendation of the American planter now-a-days that whatever pains or charge it may cost, they seldom omit to have their children instructed in reading and writing the English tongue.

William Morgan, who was born in North West Fork Hundred in Sussex County in 1780, attended such a school. The schoolhouse was built of pine slabs, and there was a hole cut in the roof to let out the smoke. There were no windows, light and air coming in through the cracks. There Morgan received instruction in reading, writing, and spelling. The

DRAUGHT

OF A

PLAN OF EDUCATION

FOR THE

WILMINGTON ACADEMY,

Which was adopted by the TRUSTEES *of the said* ACADEMY *at their Meetings on the 2d. and 22d. Day of May,* 1786.

⸺ ⸺ ⸺ ⸺

I. THE object of this Academy is to promote the important cause of Religion, Morality and Literature. For this end it is neceſſary that proper Inſtructions be furniſhed the Academicians on each of theſe Heads : Wherefore they ſhall all be ſtrictly obliged to attend every Sunday at the places of public Worſhip to which they ſeverally belong. This attendance ſhall be as punctually required, as their attendance at ſchool ; and their neglect in this caſe as ſeverely puniſhed as abſent-

ing

8-Page Draught of a Plan of Education for the Wilmington Academy, which was adopted by the Trustees of the said Academy at their meetings on the 2d. and 22d. day of May, 1786

Francis Alison: Founder and Rector of Newark Academy, 1743-1782.
Courtesy of Archives, University of Delaware.

Educational Opportunities in 1790

k bay haufe I
um, bafes be-
is plint, and
ip over dree
ihanks haufe,
i little doo—
>tter de meer
law in vorie

—————

W A R D.
e of the fub-
gh to nthip,
rs old, about
ept tired; he
ere with one
rk on the toe;
fome collar
aught horfe,
faid horfe,
ntitled to the
two dollars,

Peirce.

fhirt and trowi rs. Any perfon fecuring
him in any goal, fhall have the above reward.

Mary Bell.

October 2.

The fubfcriber intends to open an

Evening School,

At his fchool-room, on Monday the
10th Inftant.

John Thelwell.

Juft Publifhed,

And to be fold, by
Andrews, Craig, and Brynberg.
T H E

Columbian Almanac,

For the year 1791.

A LL perfons o
into flour, ar
of my improveme
at my houfe, near
the hours of four
next week.

Wilmington, O

Five
R A N away
in St. G
county, Delaw
inftant, a Negr
five feet three
fhouldered, ha
remarkable wh
old, and what
ear is off clofe
ly wears a hand
Any perfon th;
him fo that th

---

jeremian Garland.

John Kennedy,

LATELY from Europe, moft refpectfully informs his friends and the public, that he has opened S C H O O L in
New-Caftle, where he propofes to teach the
Latin and Greek Languages, Englifh Pro-
nunciation according to Sheridan. Analy-
fis and Connection according to the moft
celebrated Grammarians, as Lowth, Davis,
Buchanan, &c. in the moft *recent* and *approved* manner, and on the moft *reafonable* te ms.

New Caftle Oct. 23.   4w, 91.

Public N O T I C E.

THE fubfcriber intending to make application to the

F

W I

Burthen
She will
a great p
is a fine r
tions for
fage, app
Willing,
Philadelp

In Wilmi

The fubfcriber refpe fully informs the
Public, that he has opened a

S C H O O L,

In the HOUSE late in the poffeffion of SOLOMON
FUSSELL, where YOUTH will be inftructed in the
Englifh and French Languages, Writing,
Arithmetic, Book keeping Geography,
and the ufe of the Globes, Algebra,
Navigation, Surveying, and fuch other
Branches of Mathematics as may be
required.

*All poffible attention will be paid to the morals of the
children, and every endeavour ufed to render this School
worthy of public patronage.*

Robert Coram.

Wilmington, March 12, 1790.

a large jal
and other g
very conve
hood, and
and Wilmi
title is indi
fiderable pu
to purchafe
fubfcriber l

March 5

Juft lan
from C

J O S

A quan
Sugars,
Sole Le
Wilmin

Delaware Gazette, April 10, 1790. October 2, 1790.
November 6, 1790.

The WILMINGTON

ALMANACK,

O R

EPHEMERIS,

FOR

The Year of our LORD 1785;

Being the Firſt after LEAP-YEAR;—and the Tenth
Year of AMERICAN INDEPENDENCE.

CONTAINING

The Motions of the Sun and Moon; the true Places
and Aſpeⅽts of the Planets; the riſing and ſetting
of the Sun; and the riſing, ſetting and ſouthing of
the Moon.—*Alſo,*

The Lunations, Conjunⅽtions, Eclipſes, Judgment of
the Weather, riſing and ſetting of the Planets,
Length of Days and Nights, Fairs, Courts, Roads,
QUAKERS General Meetings, &c. Together with
uſeful Tables, chronological Obſervations, and Variety of Entertainment, in Proſe and Verſe: Among
which are,

The white Handkerchief; or, an Eſſay on Inconſtan-
cy.—No Woman without her Value: A Tale.—A
Striking Fate of Guilt.—The invincible Beauty.—
The Caſe nearly in Point: A True Tale.—Advice
to the fair Sex.—True Benevolence.—Verſes ad-
dreſſed to a modern fine Lady.—The Whole cloſed
with a laconic Sermon.

*Fitted to the Latitude of Forty Degrees, and a Meridian of
near Five Hours Weſt from London; but may, without
ſenſible Error, ſerve all the* NORTHERN COLONIES.

By THOMAS FOX, Philom.

WILMINGTON,

Printed and Sold by JAMES ADAMS.

Title page of a Wilmington Almanac, 1785.
Courtesy of Historical Society of Delaware.

J. Farrar.

POLITICAL INQUIRIES:

TO WHICH IS ADDED,

A

P L A N

FOR THE

GENERAL ESTABLISHMENT

OF

S C H O O L S

THROUGHOUT THE UNITED STATES.

BY

R O B E R T C O R A M,

*Author of some late Pieces in the Delaware Gazette, under
the Signiture of* BRUTUS.

*Above all, watch carefully over the Education of your Children. It is from
public Schools, be assured, that come the wise Magistrates—the well
trained and courageous Soldiers—the good Fathers—the good
Husbands—the good Brothers—the good Friends—the
good Men.* ——RAYNAL.

W I L M I N G T O N:

PRINTED BY ANDREWS AND BRYNBERG,
IN MARKET-STREET.

M DCC XCI.

Political Inquiries, Robert Coram.
Courtesy of the Hagley Museum and Library.

schoolmaster left after two years, and no school was held for several years. Then an old lady was hired to provide instruction in an old log house. Morgan continued in school until he was sixteen, but altogether his attendance amounted to less than two years, and his writing and spelling demonstrated the lack of instruction.

John Hamilton's experiences in attending school in Wilmington in the 1780s under a variety of masters were quite different. He probably received better instruction than did Morgan, and some of his masters such as John Filson, who prepared an early map of Kentucky, and Joseph Anderson, who became a United States Senator from Tennessee, had distinguished careers. John Thelwell, another teacher, taught three generations of Wilmington children, combining teaching with being a bellman, clerk of the markets, and many other civic responsibilities. The experiences of Morgan and Hamilton in school, along with a biography of Thelwell from Elizabeth Montgomery's reminiscences, are included in the appendix.

Robert Coram was a teacher in Wilmington, and he considered that the type of education offered in country schools throughout the United States was unsatisfactory:

> The country schools through most of the United States, whether we consider the buildings, the teachers, or the regulations, are in every respect completely despicable, wretched, and contemptible. The buildings are in general sorry hovels, neither wind tight nor water tight; a few stools serving in the double capacity of bench and desk, and the old leaves of copy books making a miserable substitute for glass windows. The teachers are generally foreigners, shamefully deficient in every good qualification necessary to convey instruction to youth, and not seldom addicted to gross vices.

Prior to the Revolution, common schools were scattered throughout the state, but none lasted for long. In Lewes, a log schoolhouse had been built on land given by John Wiltbank in 1761. The announced objective of the trustees was to see that the "youth of Sussex County be taught and educated in the Principles of Religion, Virtue and Useful Knowledge and Learning." Unfortunately, it did not turn out well, and the Anglican rector regretfully noted in 1768 that "there is not a single grammar school within the county, and it is a thing extremely rare to meet with a man who can write a tolerable hand or spell with propriety the most common words in the English language." Probably by "grammar school" in this context he had in mind a secondary school in which Latin and Greek were taught. After the Revolution the versatile Matthew Wilson, clergyman and physician, operated a school in Lewes.

A school was held in Dover in the 1760s, but the instruction was so inferior that when one of the students transferred to a Philadelphia academy he had to begin Latin over again. At the beginning of the Revolution a school was in charge of a young man who had just graduated from Newark Academy, but he remained loyal to England and received permission to travel to that country. It was on the steps of the Old Academy in Dover in 1778 that Freeborn Garretson preached the first Methodist sermon in the town. Through the combined efforts of the Anglican rector in Dover and Francis Asbury, a Methodist itinerant, a Virginian was hired in 1780 to teach school there.

In New Castle trustees of a proposed school received permission in 1772 to erect a building on a corner of the Immanuel Churchyard, but construction took place at a much later time. Temporarily the Quaker meeting house was rented for school purposes.

Friends' School in Wilmington was founded before the Revolution. Originally it was organized to provide an elementary school education in reading, writing, and ciphering for poor boys. In 1787 the curriculum was changed, and English grammar, Latin, and Greek were added to the course of instruction. According to Benjamin Ferris, Wilmington historian, this plan, except for the teaching of English grammar, did not work out because of problems concerning securing satisfactory textbooks.

Wilmington Grammar School was also founded before the Revolution. The trustees agreed upon these objectives for the institution in 1771:

> Whereas, the Town of Wilmington, aforesaid, from the pleasantness and healthiness of its situation, the plenty and goodness of its markets, and the industriousness and orderly behaviour of its inhabitants, is judged to be a fit place for erecting a publick school for the instruction of youth in the English Tongue, the Latin and Greek Languages, and in writing, arithmetic and the practical branches of mathematics, and whereas, establishing such a school on a *free and generous bottom* would not only be of great benefit to the inhabitants of the said Town, but likewise to persons at a distance, for preparing their children for a further, or collegiate education, it is therefore agreed to open such a school on the following plan. . . .

During the Revolution the use of the building by Continental and French soldiers interrupted the sessions of the school. In 1786 the trustees drew up a plan of reorganization and named the institution the Wilmington Academy. In 1787 a Mr. Freeman was hired as the professor of mathematics and of English. In addition to teaching several English and mathematics courses, he was also to give instruction in bookkeeping, geography, surveying, astronomy, and public speaking. An advertisement mentioned that he would also give lessons to young ladies in reading, grammar, writing, and "accounts." He must have been a very busy man! For a while the institution flourished, but by the end of the century the school building was converted into a manufactory. Early in the nineteenth century the school was rechartered and revived.

At the end of the eighteenth century parents were very

conscious of the importance of education for their children and willing to make sacrifices for this purpose. In 1797 a group of persons interested in education raised money to build a school near Brandywine Bridge on land donated by John Welsh and John Dickinson. More than four hundred dollars was raised in subscriptions. The preamble to the subscription list made clear why parents and friends of education were willing to donate funds:

> We, the undersigned, subscribers of Brandywine Hundred and County of New Castle, considering the utility of schools or seminaries of learning and being willing and desirous to promote the building of a schoolhouse within our neighbourhood, or district, for the comfortable accommodation of our children and those who may be employed in their tuition there, we, the said subscribers, hereunto severally promise . . .

Francis Alison, an influential Presbyterian clergyman, founded a school in New London, Pennsylvania in 1742, which was moved to Newark prior to the Revolution and renamed Newark Academy. In 1769 the institution received a charter from Thomas and Richard Penn. About this time, Dr. Alison, who had become vice-provost of the College of Philadelphia but retained an interest in the academy, mentioned that sixty boys were in attendance, studying language, mathematics, and logic. Parents were assured in advertisements such as one appearing in the *Pennsylvania Journal* in 1771 that Newark was a highly moral town and that instruction by tutors of decent deportment and approved virtue was conducted under the watchful eyes of the trustees. "The small town of New Ark," the advertisement mentioned, "which is generally inhabited by sober, industrious people, affords no public amusements, nor any remarkable instances of profligacy and vice to draw the attention of youth, divert them from their studies, or turn them aside from the paths of virtue." Some students at Newark Academy probably attained the goal mentioned in a poem written in 1772 glorifying the virtues of life along the banks of White Clay Creek and published in the *Pennsylvania Gazette:*

And with New Ark I will live,
Whilst her plains these pleasures give,
Till my youthful notions rise,
Clad with ancient Wisdom's Guise.

NEWARK ACADEMY BOARDING RATES, 1787

The Trustees of the ACADEMY of Newark finding, That notwithstanding those Advantages which have rendered the Seminary of Learning so justly celebrated, such as the remarkable healthfulness of the Place, the decent and orderly Behaviour of the Inhabitants, and the great Care which has always been taken that the Tutors should be well qualified for the important Trust, of which the Present Tutor, Mr. WILLIAM THOMPSON, is an eminent example; yet the Price of Twenty-five Pounds per Annum which has been generally taken for Boarding, when Cash is so scarce, has discouraged several from sending their Children there for Education:----The Trustees, therefore, having earnestly recommended to the Inhabitants to lower their Prices, have the Satisfaction to inform the PUBLIC, that the Inhabitants have cheerfully agreed to board, wash and lodge hereafter, the Children sent there for Education, at the Rate of Eighteen Pounds per Annum, to be paid in half-yearly Payments.-----Tuition to be Five Pounds per Annum as usual.

JOHN THOMPSON, Sec'ry.

Newark, June 25, 1787
Delaware Courant, July 14, 1787 (Microfilm)

During the Revolution, the march of the British through Newark disrupted the school, and its funds, which had been

taken to Wilmington, were captured. The structure in which
the school met was converted into a shoe factory for the
Continental Army. The school probably reopened in 1780.
The curriculum apparently continued to emphasize English
grammar, mathematics, and ancient languages. Declining en-
rollments were a problem. In 1787 the trustees announced
that in spite of Newark being celebrated for its healthfulness,
the orderly behavior of the inhabitants, and careful selection
of the tutors, some parents hesitated to send their sons to the
academy because of the high price of room and board. Consequently, the trustees had arranged with the inhabitants to
fix the price of room, board, and washing at eighteen pounds
per annum rather than twenty-five pounds, though tuition
remained fixed at five pounds. The school was temporarily
closed from 1796 to 1799, and then reopened.

Many other types of schools flourished in Delaware, especially in Wilmington, for short times in the last part of the
eighteenth century. Schoolmasters such as Robert Coram,
John Thelwell, and William Cobbett, the English essayist,
politician, and agriculturist, often advertised in Wilmington
newspapers. On one occasion Thelwell offered to teach black
students in the evening, free of charge. Young women could
receive instruction from Mrs. Chappell in paper filigree work,
and Mrs. Cooke opened a boarding school for girls in 1799.
In the 1790s students had opportunities to attend special
schools of dance, fencing, music, and singing. In 1781 Fred
Jordan offered to provide instruction for children of either sex
in writing, reading, and arithmetic. Opportunities for education in small towns and rural areas were limited. In 1790
John Kennedy opened a school in New Castle and conducted
classes in English grammar, Latin, Greek, and mathematics.

A select group of residents, especially those living in
Wilmington, had an interest in culture, science, and intellec-
tual matters. They were the people who patronized Wilmington and Philadelphia bookstores and whose names appeared
on the subscription list to the *American Museum,* a magazine
which began publication in Philadelphia in the 1780s. Judg-

Title page from a Wilmington Almanac, 1797.
Courtesy of Historical Society of Delaware.

ing from the small size of Wilmington and the number of
bookstores, the town was more intellectually oriented then
than it is today.

Bookstores in Wilmington offered printed materials for
every taste—history, essays, magazines, novels, travel books,
and sermons. Some publications had special appeal to women.

s Employ,

Nurfe,

ake a child in, or go
quire of the Printers.

SOLD.

ry BRICK HOUSE
us back buildings; fituate
ton, adjoining the houfes of
s, the whole complete; £.
£ 45 per annum. The lot
Market ftreet, and extends
eet, on which are two fmall
nting at £ 8 per annum,
t without the houfe, as may
he whole is clear of ground
be made eafy.   For furthe

OBERT TAYLOR

T E D,
ced Miller,
will meet with good encou-
Chriftiana-Bridge, to
OSEPH ISRAEL

the Printing-Office
ITY of

edicines,

TY; of which are,
ots Pills, Hooper's
Oil, Britifh ditto,
affy's Elixir, God-
ington's Balfam of

L I S H E D,
Printers hereof, the
l Government,

JUST PUBLISHED,
And to be fold by the Printers hereof,
T H E
DELAWARE & FEDERAL

ALMANACS,

For the Year 1790.
Containing, the Motions of the Sun and
Moon, the true Places and Afpects of
the Planets, the Rifing and Setting of
the Sun, the Rifing, Setting and Southing of the Moon, the Lunations, Con-
junctions, and Eclipfes, the Rifing,
Setting and Southing of the Planets,
Length of Days, Judgment of the
Weather, Feftivals, and other remarkable Days ; likewife Quakers Yearly
Meetings ; alfo Fairs, Courts, Roads,
&c. &c. entertaining Remarks, with
an Ode on Humanity---authentic In-
ftance of the horrid Barbarity of re-
licous Perfecution --a curious Fact---
fingular Cuftom in the Ifle of Man---
Anecdotes of Dean Swift---the Policy
of Phyficians---furprifing Anecdote of
a Dog---Rhapfody on Indolence---
Anti-airbaloon----remarkable American Occurrences---a Recipe for pre-
venting Flies from damaging the
feeding Leaves of Turneps, Cabbages,
Radifhes and many other Vegetables
---Receipt for the Cure of a Pain in
the Stomach, attended with a fevere
Griping---an effectual Remedy for
that awful Malady the Cancer---Scale
of Depreciation, for the Settlement of
Debts--Table of the Value of Weights
and Coins as they now pafs in England, Pennfylvania and New-York,
&c.

Six Dollars Reward.

R AN away from the fubfcriber, liv-

Books for Sale.
Delaware Gazette, September 30, 1789.

ppears that the king of
ed in some of the prints ,
ay of recovery from his
ich, the appointment of a
ninistry, had not taken
ritish plenipotentiary at
st concluded a treaty of
catholic majesty. That
nder the command of the
Constantinople, and pla-
rnwallis, governor-gene-
s, had impeached a num-
l-administration in that
vill be sent to England for

March 21.

is accosted on Saturday
rristiana bridge, by a man
ield a little distance out
lling a horse. He there
y the fence, and a horse
ed him by the leg, and
deliver, he would blow
on told them he supposed
anted, but desired leave
hich he had no sooner
ne would not be robbed.
him with couteau knives;
ition from a stick which
ter a smart engagement,
nd rode off through the

d in this port, the brig
wn, in 20 days from St.

ors of South-Carolina and
ppears that that illustrious
George Washington, esq.
President of the United

of the Royal Academy
g of savages, makes the
r and *nouvelle* remarks :
us in all the qualities of
ceptible. Their faces are
ian ours, if they did not
ing, and false ornaments.
eir knowledge, but they
e and reflection, and are
heart, they are said, here
d cruel, but I do not be-
n such. The custom of
ge nations, does not pro-
th, which, after all, can-
l, or morally speaking,
other animal flesh. When
and society must lose a
whether he be hanged,
aten. Infants are worse
hrown into the river like
d with them. Nav. they

JUST PUBLISHED,
And to be had of
JAMES ADAMS,
At his Printing-Office, in Wilmington, the
LAWS,
Passed at the last session of the General Assembly of the
Delaware state ; among which is an act for regulat-
ing and establishing the fees of all the public of-
ficers of the state, from the highest to the lowest in
office.
Of whom also may be had, the following books, viz.

BURKET on the New-
Testament
Cruden's Concordance
Brown's Dictionary of the
Bible
Bates on Man's Redemption
Edwards on Original Sin
Brown's Exposition of the
Epistle of Paul to the
Romans
Tennent's twenty four
Sermons on the chief
end of Man
Bishop Beveridge's body of
Divinity
Watson's body of divini-
ty
Edwards's history of Re-
demption
Ditto on the Affections
Pattillo's Sermons, and
Advice to Husbands and
Wives, Children and
Servants
Religious Courtship
Guthrie's and Salmon's
Geographical Grammar
History of sir Charles Gran-
dison, in a series of Let-
ters, 8 vols.
Spectator, 8 vols.
Adventurer, 4 vols.
Rambler, 6 vols.
New Roman History by
question and answer
Martin's, Paley's and Ni-
cholson's Philosophy
Hammond's Algebra
Atkinson's epitomy of the
art of Navigation
Art of Speaking
Lord Chesterfield's advice
to his son, on men and
manners, being a new
system of Education
The Beauties of History, or
Pictures of Virtue and
Vice, drawn from real
life, 2 vols.

The Children's Friend
Percival's Father's Instruc-
tions, consisting of mo-
ral tales, fables and re-
flections
Defence of Theron and
Aspasio
Constitutions of the thir-
teen United States of
America
Songs, comic and satyri-
cal, by George A. Ste-
vens
Markham and Bartlet's
Farriery
Virgil
Greek and Latin Lexicon
French Grammar, and
other French school-
books
German ditto.
School Bibles
Testaments
Dilworth's Schoolmaster's
Assistant
Fisher's Arithmetic
Young Man's Companion
Spelling-Books
Different kinds of primers,
and small books for
children
Writing Paper
Blank-Books
Variety of Plays
American Museum, from
its commencement to
the close of 1788, neatly
bound and lettered, in
4 vols.
Best Ink-Powder
Wafers
Blank-Books
Bonds
Bills of Loading
Arbitration Bonds
Shipping Bills
Apprentices and Servants
Indentures, &c. &c.

POE

A SUBUR

A Reverend de
   About who
   Thus for hi
" Have patience-v
With joy-prick'd
And deem'd the d
On his first head
They sat with pat
" And now," say
" Great is your p
" T'abuse that no
" So I'll defer it t

Anecdote o

IN the heat of t
   off his head, a
began to give
Cossacks and Cal
them, " I order
away, and to kill
fame." The cons
to the advanced g
self, gained that
Charles XII's gran
vegred, and his t
thing to fire and s
ous of his men, a
hands ; and havi
fellows, he went t
ran to shelter then
upon the table, fa
inhabitants it is c
own soldiers, whi

THE W
open on the
in the aftern
next, where atte

3d mo. 21st, 17

Lan

TO be SOL
   Wednesda
ing, Kent
Tracts of LAN
Bourbon county, d
The title indisput

Books for Sale.
Delaware Gazette, March 21, 1789.

Children could buy slates, Dilworth's books on arithmetic, English grammar, and bookkeeping, and enjoyable volumes like *Goody Two Shoes,* now a treasured item in the Dorman collection in the Historical Society of Delaware. For earthy humor one might select *Funny Stories; or The American Jester, being a companion for a merry good fellow, containing funny anecdotes, wise sayings and smart repartee,* published in Wilmington in 1797. The jokes and anecdotes are so robust that it is doubtful that they would be related in mixed company, and it was difficult to make a selection to appear in the appendix.

Few young men attended college. Exceptions were Dr. James Tilton of Dover and Dr. Nicholas Way of Wilmington, who were among the first graduates of the medical school of the College of Philadelphia in 1768. George Monro studied medicine at Edinburgh University. If young men did seek for a higher education, they usually enrolled at the College of Philadelphia or at the College of New Jersey (later Princeton). John Dickinson went overseas to study law in the Inns of Court in London. More commonly, men acquired a knowledge of law by reading and by the observation of professional men who acted as their preceptors. This was the method used by Thomas McKean and George Read to study law.

The inventories of most people's possessions contained no references to books other than to a Bible and prayer book. But there are many exceptions. John Dickinson took pride in his fine library. Dr. Charles Ridgely owned over one hundred volumes, including many volumes in Latin and a few in Greek and French. Dr. Matthew Wilson of Lewes possessed a library of one hundred volumes in history, literature, religion, and medicine. Daniel Nunez of Lewes, who once had been the sheriff of Sussex County and an innkeeper, had more than fifty legal volumes in his library of one hundred books. An outstanding library was owned by Chief Justice Vining of Dover, who died in 1770. He had collected more than two hundred well-selected books—travel, history, law, drama, essays—of which any gentleman in the American colonies would have been proud. The inventory of a Wilmington printer, James Adams, at the time of his death in 1793, contained more than one hundred volumes listed by title, sometimes in multiple copies, plus 3,600 unbound "testaments."

The Wilmington Library Company was formed by a group of gentleman of New Castle County and chartered by the legislature in 1788. John Dickinson headed the list of organizers, including some of the most cultured and influential men in Wilmington and the vicinity. The library contained more than three hundred carefully selected volumes of high quality. The names of the charter members and the titles of these volumes are printed in the appendix.

Some Delawareans, such as John Dickinson, Thomas McKean, John Vining, Charles Ridgely, William Poole, James Tilton, and Nicholas Way, belonged to the American Philosophical Society. Francis Alison, founder of Newark Academy, and Charles Thomson, formerly of Delaware, secretary of the Continental Congress, were members. These were truly men of distinction, and most of them had a variety of interests. Dickinson, McKean, and Vining were active in politics, law, and government.

Dr. Matthew Wilson was a clergyman and a physician, living at Lewes, outside of this circle. A staunch supporter of the American cause in the Revolution, he named his son James Patriot Wilson and wore a tricornered hat bearing on one side the word "liberty." He compiled an alphabetical list of diseases and their treatment. A scholar who studied the medical history of Delaware declared that if the manuscript of over three hundred pages had been published, it would have been the first volume on the practice of medicine (other than surgery) printed by an American author.

Thomas Rodney, who studied religion, philosophy, mythology, geography, government, history, and science, had one of the most inquisitive minds in the state. He was greatly interested in the transit of Venus in 1769, discussing it in Dover with Dr. Tilton; John Vining, the son of the chief justice; Dr. Mark McCall, a school teacher; and Dr. Charles

Ridgely. With the latter, Rodney also conversed about the effects of drinking on one's health and about vaccination. Some of Rodney's ideas are not accepted today. For example, he believed that white men originated in frigid climates, black men in tropical climates, and brown men in temperate climates. He thought that the planets were inhabited by men similar to those on earth. He claimed that God had created the universe, earth, and man. Rodney composed a letter to Thomas Jefferson on these topics, but it is uncertain whether it was mailed.

One of the results of the American Revolution was to open wider the doors of scientific and philosophical inquiry. In his letter to Jefferson, Rodney wrote:

> The Revolution of America by recognizing these rights which every Man is entitled to by the Laws of God and nature seems to have broke off those devious tramels of Ignorance, Prejudice and Superstition which have long depressed the Human Mind. Every door is now open to the sons of genius and science to enquire after Truth. Hence we may expect the darkening clouds of error will vanish fast before the light of reason; and that the period is fast arriving when the Truth will enlighten the whole world.

Let us hope that the school system in the eighteenth century contributed to terminating ignorance, prejudice, and superstition and laid the foundations for establishing methods by which to arrive at the truth.

VIII ──────────────────────── RELIGION

The religious heritage of the state reflected the diverse backgrounds of the settlers. The desire for religious freedom had been the principal motivation for many to emigrate to the New World. On the eve of the American Revolution, the colony of Delaware contained twenty-nine Presbyterian churches, twelve Anglican, twelve Quaker, one Lutheran, and one Baptist. While nominally most of the inhabitants were considered to be Anglican, services were not well attended, and only five Anglican clergymen ministered to the spiritual needs of the inhabitants. Thomas McKean believed that the Anglican Church had its greatest strength in Kent and Sussex counties.

Examination of the position of the Anglican Church in Kent County demonstrates how weak it was. In 1762 the population of Kent County was estimated to be about seven thousand, with one-sixth of the total being Anglican and slightly more than one-sixth composed of dissenters such as Presbyterians, Quakers, Nicholites, and a few Catholics. Only a small number of Anglicans took communion at any time, in part because according to the *Book of Common Prayer* communicants were supposed to be confirmed by a bishop, and no Anglican bishop ever visited America. A recent study of religion on the Delmarva Peninsula estimates that two-thirds of the population of Kent County were unchurched in the late colonial period. The rector of the Dover church probably understated the situation in 1760 when he reported that there

110

were several hundred people in the county "who perhaps have never heard a sermon and do not belong to any religious denomination of Christians." This clergyman was referring especially to the residents of the "forest" along the Maryland border west of Dover and also to those who lived in the marshes east of the county seat.

The Presbyterian Church had many members in New Castle County, where many of the inhabitants had come from northern Ireland. Thomas McKean believed that this denomination, with seventeen churches, contained more members than any other. But in the entire county, in 1776, there were only four Presbyterian ministers.

Other denominations had smaller memberships in Delaware. In spite of the efforts of William Penn, Quakers remained a minority. Wilmington was founded by Quakers, and they remained influential members of the community in economic and cultural life. More Quaker meeting houses were located in New Castle County than in Kent and Sussex counties. Old Swedes Church, the only Lutheran church in the colony, was a heritage of earlier days. Prior to the Revolution, the Baptists had founded one church, located in the Welsh Tract near Newark. The spiritual needs of the few Catholics were looked after by priests who came over from Maryland to conduct services in private homes. Sometimes inventories of deceased persons' possessions provided evidence that a person was Catholic. At the time of her death in 1772, Sarah Darby of Sussex County owned a volume entitled *History of the Catholick Church*. In 1772, Catholics purchased a tract of land at Coffee Run in northern New Castle County on which to construct a mission chapel, though it was not constructed until many years later. Methodist evangelists had appeared in the colony prior to the Revolution. George Whitefield first came in 1739 and returned several times. With his preachings he helped establish a pattern of revivalism later used effectively.

The Revolution had distinct effects upon some of these

Friends' Second Meeting house built 1748.
Taken down in 1817.

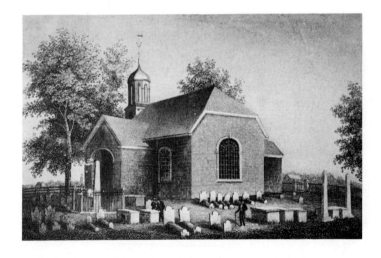

Old Swedes Church.

First Presbyterian Meeting House, Wilmington, Delaware.
Founded 1740.

Barratt's Chapel.
Picture Collection, Historical Society of Delaware.

denominations. The Anglican Church became discredited because the rectors and members were accused of wishing to remain loyal to England. The rector at Appoquinimink closed his church in 1776 and never officiated at services there again. But the other Anglican clergymen in the colony managed to continue to hold services, even after the legislature declared that it was an act of treason to pray for the king and the royal family of Great Britain. By the end of the war, one clergyman had moved to Virginia, another to Philadelphia, two had died, and only one continued to perform his clerical duties. After the war the Anglican Church in the United States was reorganized and adopted the name of Protestant Episcopal. But the denomination never regained the place of prominence that it had held before the Revolution. Old Swedes Church joined this denomination.

During the Revolution and immediately thereafter the Baptist Church grew until by 1791 the denomination consisted of nine churches with a membership of 380 persons. But some of these churches disappeared early in the nineteenth century.

Quakers were treated badly by both sides during the war. They refused to serve in the militia or the Delaware Regiment, pay taxes to support the war, or to accept Continental currency. The Quakers of Duck Creek Meeting in 1785 summed up some of their difficulties in that troublesome period, declaring:

And whereas our Ancient Testimony being against joining in with, pulling down, or setting up Governments, many of us found ourselves religiously bound in support of this Testimony, from having anything to do with the Government in the unsettled state thereof during the late commotions, even to use it on any occasion; whereby, some were sufferers illegally and sought no remedy therefore, this restraint extended to refuse active compliance to contribute to the support thereof by payment of taxes demanded for that purpose.

At the end of the war, Quakers remained, just as at its beginning, a small influential minority, particularly in business, education, and commerce in Wilmington.

An interesting small sect in Delaware was the Nicholites, founded by Joseph Nichols of Kent County in about the middle of the eighteenth century. His indebtedness to the Quakers was shown by his emphasis on the "Inner Light" as a means of grace, on simplicity of dress and living, on pacificism, and abolition of slavery. It was natural that his followers should be referred to as "Friends" or the "New Quakers." The movement spread from the Maryland-Delaware border to Guilford County in North Carolina and also to one area of South Carolina. Following Nichols' death about 1774, the movement became more organized, but gradually the members joined the Quaker faith. By 1800 the sect had virtually disappeared.

Following the war, the Presbyterians continued to be stronger in New Castle County than elsewhere in the state. Scotch-Irish immigration continued, and the denomination grew in numbers.

The first Catholic church, a log structure, was built at Coffee Run in 1790 and named St. Mary's of the Assumption. In the 1790s an influx of refugees came from Santo Domingo into Wilmington, and the need for a Catholic church in that city became evident. This need was reinforced after the turn of the century with the arrival of Irish immigrants, some of whom worked in the Du Pont powder mills.

The most striking religious change during the Revolution and immediately thereafter was in the number of Methodists. On the eve of the war, Methodist itinerants had just begun to preach in the colony. In spite of the fact that John Wesley supported the British government and that Methodists in America were sometimes accused of being opposed to separation from the mother country, the denomination grew in popularity. A study of the Methodists on the Delmarva Peninsula lists 253 Methodists in 1775, and 4,604 in 1784, the latter figure being practically six percent of the population. The number of circuits in that period grew from one to seven, and the number of itinerants from two to seventeen. By 1784 there were at least twenty Methodist houses of worship. Through weekly meetings of small groups under a leader, the spiritual condition of members was carefully supervised.

At first, Methodists remained members of the Anglican Church. The only way that a minister could be ordained was to travel to England to have this function performed by a bishop. Because of the urgent need for Methodist ministers, John Wesley tried unsuccessfully to have the ordination process changed so that it might take place in America. He then decided that the Methodists in America must achieve some kind of independence. Thomas Coke was sent to carry this message to America, and he and Asbury were to be joint superintendents or bishops. At Barratt's Chapel near Frederica, the "Cradle of Methodism," Coke met Asbury and revealed Wesley's plans to him. A conference at Baltimore established a separate denomination. Whether Wesley had intended this, or meant only for the American Methodists to have some degree of autonomy, is uncertain.

Methodism had a special appeal to slaves and free blacks, perhaps because it emphasized the conversion experience more than religious instruction, and followed the position of Wesley in opposing slavery. The enthusiasm evident in the lively services also had appeal. In 1787, blacks numbered 1,839 or thirty percent of all Delmarva Methodists. By 1793 the total number of black Methodists was 3,549.

In retrospect, the 1780s were a time when great religious changes were taking place in the state, with the decline in importance of the Anglican Church and the rise of Methodism.

IX — GOVERNMENT AND POLITICS

Politically the 1780s were a difficult period. Physical violence was sometimes evident at elections. The war was dragging to a close, and the state owed money to the national treasury, to veterans, and to many citizens who had supplied goods or services. Peace in 1783—long looked forward to—did not result in prosperity and a golden age, as many had anticipated; instead came heavy taxes and foreclosures of mortgages because farmers were not receiving enough money from the sale of crops to meet their debts. Continental and state currency was in disarray. All of these problems, and many others, called for action by the General Assembly and for a display of wisdom, which was not always forthcoming.

In the 1780s the state was governed under a constitution framed in 1776. This document had established an upper house called the Legislative Council and a lower house named the House of Assembly. The members were mostly farmers and landowners with a sprinkling of lawyers, physicians, and flour millers. The lower house served as a training ground for politicians who might later be elected to the upper house or to state or national office. The Legislative Council specialized in proposing amendments and revisions to bills submitted by the lower house. In addition to these two bodies, the constitution also provided for a president (governor) as the chief executive with limited powers. Some of his duties were carried on with the aid of a Privy Council of four

members, two being elected by each house. The constitution
also set up a system of courts.

In the 1780s the leadership in the General Assembly was
changing. Undoubtedly the most influential person in the legislature was George Read, who served in that body before
and during the Revolution, as well as in the Continental
Congress and later was a member of the Annapolis and
Philadelphia conventions. Even after he was elected to serve
in the United States Senate in 1788, he continued to be
consulted about legislative matters. Thomas McKean, who
had been very active in Delaware politics before the Revolution and in its early years, was now involved in governmental
affairs in Pennsylvania, becoming chief justice and later governor of that state. Caesar Rodney, who had completed his
term as president of the Delaware state in 1781, was in feeble
health and died in 1784. Thus, the way was open for new
leadership, but the men who came forward as speakers of the
two houses, members of Congress, and governors were not
of the same caliber as Read, McKean, and Rodney, even
though they were able and conscientious administrators. Not
until James A. Bayard came forward as a member of Congress
in 1797 and began a family dynasty in the Senate in 1805 did
the state again have a nationally known political leader.

Party alignment in the 1780s was between factions rather
than between well-organized parties. At the beginning of the
Revolution in 1775 and 1776, those who came to favor
independence from Great Britain and were willing to fight for
it were commonly called Whigs, and those in opposition,
who were more hesitant about separation and going to war,
were called Tories. Some historians of the Revolution prefer
to use the terms "radicals" instead of Whig and "moderates" or "conservatives" instead of Tory. Those Americans
who joined the British forces, sold supplies to the British,
and provided helpful information were called "loyalists." In
this study we have decided to continue to use the term Whig,
but prefer to use moderate or conservative to describe the
attitudes of many Delawareans who did not jump whole-

heartedly on the band wagon in support of independence. Certainly we do not regard such political leaders as George Read, John Dickinson, and Dr. John McKinly, the state's first president, as disloyal in any sense, though they were not hotheads like Caesar Rodney and Thomas McKean at the beginning of the Revolution. The people of Delaware appreciated and understood the moderate stands of Read, Dickinson, and McKinly and rewarded them with high office.

Delaware governors corresponded with the chief executives of other states about common problems. At the suggestion of Virginia a conference was summoned to meet in Annapolis, Maryland, in September 1786 to discuss commerical relations. The Delaware General Assembly selected John Dickinson, Richard Bassett, George Read, Jacob Broom, and Gunning Bedford, Jr. as delegates to the conference. The first three men were well-known politicians, while Broom was a Wilmington businessman and Bedford was the state's attorney general.

When the Annapolis convention met, it did little because it was poorly attended. Delaware was represented by Dickinson, Read, and Bassett. Dickinson was chosen chairman and signed the final report, which proposed that a convention meet in Philadelphia in May to "revise" the Articles of Confederation.

Delaware's General Assembly chose the same five delegates to attend the Philadelphia convention. Under the guidance of George Read, a member of the Legislative Council, instructions to the Delaware delegates directed them to seek equality with all other states in any legislative body that might be set up by the Philadelphia convention.

Of the Delaware delegation Dickinson and Read had the most impact upon the deliberations of the Philadelphia convention. They were particularly watchful that the instructions of the legislature were observed. In a compromise, equality of representation was secured in the United States Senate, though the representation in the House of Representatives was according to population. The work of the Philadelphia convention was completed on September 17, and the document was signed by members of the Delaware delegation, except for the absent Dickinson, who gave his friend George Read permission to sign for him.

Now it was time for the legislatures of the states to arrange for conventions to consider the proposed constitution. The people of Delaware were predisposed to approve the document. An article in the *Delaware Courant*, dated Wilmington, September 7, 1787, declared:

> We learn from Philadelphia "that the Convention propose to adjourn next week, after laying America under such obligations to them for their long, painful and disinterested labours, to establish her liberty upon a permanent basis as no time will ever cancel."

Along with a controversial election in Sussex County, almost the entire time of the General Assembly meeting in October was taken up with this matter. Even before the General Assembly met, several petitions from New Castle County urged "speedy" action in arranging for a convention and recommended approval of the constitution. As soon as a sufficient number of members were present to form a quorum, President Thomas Collins on October 24 presented a message recommending careful consideration of the document, as even the "national existence" of the United States might be at stake. The two houses had no particular disagreement about arranging for a convention of thirty members, ten from each county, to meet in Dover, beginning on December 3, to consider the document. Instructions from the legislature to the delegates also recommended that they consider offering land in Delaware to the national government as a site for the national capital. Election of the members of the Constitutional Convention would take place on November 26.

The members of the legislature more easily disposed of arrangements for the convention than they did of the disputed Sussex County election. For ten days an investigation was carried on, and the sheriff, subsheriff, and numerous witnesses were asked to testify. Gradually a picture of disorder, riots, and confusion emerged on the day of the election. The sheriff had postponed its being held from day to day because of disturbances such as the appearance of companies of "associators," mostly veterans, who were armed with clubs, pistols, and swords and bore colorful flags. President Collins visited Sussex County and arranged that an election be held on October 15 of a Union ticket composed of an equal number from each opposing faction. Only fifty persons from each party would be permitted to vote. On that day minor rioting occurred, but, on the whole, violence was kept within bounds. After investigation the legislature declared that the returns were invalid and directed that another election be held on November 26. On the same day voters were to choose the members to attend the convention at Dover to consider the federal constitution. The site of the election was moved by action of the legislature from Lewes, a Whig stronghold, to the home of Robert Griffith near Vaughan's Furnace in the center of the county, an area inhabited largely by conservatives and moderates. Returns from the election for members of the General Assembly would be submitted to the legislature in January, 1788.

While the election on November 26 passed off peacefully in New Castle and Kent counties, this was not so in Sussex County. Petitions came from Sussex County claiming that companies of armed men stationed near the polling place prevented Whigs from voting and intimidated many voters. A prejudiced Whig commentator, "Timoleon" (Dr. James Tilton), reported that upon that occasion "sundry persons were insulted and violently assaulted professedly because they were Whigs, Presbyterians, or Irish-men; that one fellow in particular, after assaulting a Whig with several blows, swore his teeth had grown an inch on that day that he might *eat* Presbyterians and Irish-men; that some huzzaed for the King, and others expressed a hope that they might again come under the old government." But neither side was interested in delaying the work of the convention. Moreover, the members felt that they lacked authority to send for witnesses and to conduct an investigation into the election. Under these circumstances the members from Sussex County were seated in the convention. In January, 1788, after deliberations, the legislature also decided to seat the moderate members elected to the House of Assembly and the one member to the Legislative Council.

The Constitutional Convention that met in Dover on Monday, December 3, 1787, in Battell's tavern, consisted of thirty members. The composition of the body was much like that of the General Assembly, consisting mainly of farmers and landowners, with some physicians, lawyers, and grist mill owners. Many of the members had served as officers in the state militia or in the Delaware Regiment, and others had been members of the General Assembly in the past or held other political offices. President Collins submitted a brief message to the members and presented them with a copy of the federal constitution. He also provided copies of the instructions passed by the General Assembly about the convention and called attention to the section recommending that a site within the state be offered for the national capital. Unfortunately, little is known about the deliberations of this body, as the minutes have not survived. The members of the convention ratified the constitution unanimously, and all thirty delegates signed the form of ratification on December 7, known today as Delaware Day. The members of the convention also agreed to offer a site within the state to Congress for a national capital.

Delaware's ratification of the constitution was widely reported in the newspapers. A Massachusetts newspaper headed an article about Delaware's initiative, "The FIRST PILLAR of a great FEDERAL SUPERSTRUCTURE raised." Pennsylvania followed on December 12, and New Jersey on December 18. Delaware, with her Delaware Valley neighbors, had blazed a trail, which other states followed.

Convention Ordered to be Held

WILMINGTON, October 31. On Monday, the 22nd last agreeable to Law, the General Assembly of this State met at Dover, but a sufficient number of the members not attending, the house adjourned from day to day till Wednesday, when a quorum being present, the House of Assembly proceeded to business and elected Thomas Rodney, Esquire, Speaker, and James Booth, Esq., Clerk. They then ordered a Convention to be called for taking into consideration the plan of government recommended by the late Federal Convention; the election to be held at the usual place in each County, on the third Monday of this month; and the Convention to meet at Dover on the next Monday thereafter.

Some of the members chosen for Sussex attended, but the Sheriff not having made any return, they did not take their seats.

Delaware Courant, October 31, 1787.

Why was Delaware the first state to ratify the Constitution? No one reason explains this, but a number were involved. Sentiment in the state was so much in favor of the Constitution that the General Assembly was disappointed in late August when the work of the federal convention was not yet completed, and the legislature could not proceed to arrange for a state constitutional convention. Many Delawareans believed that a stronger government might solve many of the problems with which the Confederation Congress had not dealt. The Wilmington business community, which had close relations with Philadelphia, favored approval, and it is significant that several petitions signed by businessmen and others in its favor came from New Castle County. Some Delawareans hoped that the location of the national capital might be in the state. Moreover, there was great respect and admiration for George Washington, who presided at the deliberations.

Both Whigs and moderates in Delaware supported ratification. An Anti-Federalist party did not appear in the state. Why did the leading political factions in Delaware support ratification? Probably the explanation is that political leaders of the two principal factions believed that chaos and confusion in state and local affairs should not continue. A stronger government could face foreign nations, regulate commerce, provide a sound currency, and establish order more effectively than the existing Congress. In a partisan political pamphlet published in 1788, Timoleon (Dr. James Tilton) put the matter this way in a conclusion: "Although every other means under Providence should fail us, we hope at least to derive some consolation from the NEW FEDERAL CONSTITUTION. From hence we may expect some standing institutions to walk by." Members of both political factions could have subscribed to this sentiment.

It was probably the example of the Articles of Confederation being replaced by the federal Constitution that inspired political leaders in the state to undertake the revision of the state constitution of 1776. At the request of a majority of the members of the House of Assembly, President Joshua Clayton convened a special session of the legislature on September 5, 1791, to consider calling a convention to revise the state constitution or to frame a new one. Within three days the General Assembly had completed its work. Resolutions were passed to the effect that the general departments of the government were "blended together" and poorly arranged, that the burdens and expenses of the government were borne with difficulty, and that in some instances the provisions of the Delaware constitution were in conflict with the federal Constitution. The members issued a call for the election of thirty persons, ten from each county, to meet in Dover on Tuesday, November 29, to undertake this work.

The convention was composed of the same kind of persons who were elected to the General Assembly—farmers, landowners, physicians, grist mill owners, and merchants. The elected chairman was John Dickinson, who at that time resided primarily in Wilmington. After he resigned as chairman because of ill health, he was replaced by another delegate from New Castle County named Thomas Montgomery. One of the interesting members of the convention was Robert Coram of Wilmington, a teacher and at one time editor of a Wilmington newspaper. He had written a pamphlet about government which may have had some influence in having the convention called.

In the first session, which lasted until the end of December, the members examined the government system of the state and found it to be deficient and inadequate. Therefore they decided to prepare a new constitution. This document provided for a governor with increased powers, a more clear-cut division among the legislative, executive, and judicial branches, and more participation by the people in the election process. The members adjourned on December 31 and submitted this document to citizens for examination and criticism. The body would meet again on May 29, 1792, to consider changes.

In a two-week session in the early summer the members made many changes, but they failed to act upon requests from Quakers to abolish slavery and to exempt persons from military duty who were opposed to war on religious grounds. The twenty-three members who were present on June 12, the day of adjournment, signed the constitution, and it went immediately into effect without being submitted to the people of the state for a vote of approval.

The new constitution resembled in some ways the federal Constitution because of the presence of John Dickinson and Richard Bassett, who had served as members of the Philadelphia convention. As in the federal government, the upper and lower houses were now called the house of representatives and senate. The name of the state was changed from Delaware State to the State of Delaware.

Article I contained a bill of rights of nineteen provisions, which was mostly a rewriting of the Declaration of Rights of the Delaware Constitution of 1776. Article II dealt with the powers of the legislature composed of the senate of nine members and of the house of representatives of twenty-two members. The General Assembly was to meet on the first Tuesday in January, rather than in October, with elections being held in November. In counties, voters elected annually seven members of the lower house and one to the upper house, biennially a member of the national House of Representatives, and triennially a governor and two candidates for sheriff and for coroner, of which one was selected for office by the head of the executive branch. Article III described the powers of the chief executive, whose title was changed from president to governor. Henceforth he was to be elected by the people rather than by the legislature. While his powers were somewhat enlarged, he still lacked the veto power. This constitution, which increased the powers of the governor and was more democratic than its predecessor, served the state well for more than a third of a century, until it was replaced in 1831.

X ——————————— IN RETROSPECT

In the early 1780s came many changes. The war with Great Britain ended at last. Veterans returned home and found that residents who had remained in the state and opposed or been indifferent to independence now wished to share in its benefits. Clashes between these factions were frequent at polling places in Kent and Sussex counties. Farmers complained in petitions to the legislature of the low prices for grain and the scarcity of money. The academies in Newark and in Wilmington were reorganized.

Gradually the times became better, especially in the Wilmington area. A new spirit of enterprise flourished in the town in the late 1780s and early 1790s. While the Brandywine flour mills continued to be the most important element in the economy, shipbuilding revived and Jacob Broom briefly opened a cotton textile mill on the Brandywine. Merchants found it profitable to ship flour and breadstuffs to the West Indies and sometimes along the coast. Imports consisted of British hardware and textiles as well as tropical products, coffee, and spices. By 1790 the town had a population of about two thousand. The first newspaper of which we have any issues was published in the town, and the Library Company of Wilmington was chartered by the legislature. New Castle County farmers found a good market for wheat, agricultural produce, and cattle here.

Downstate changes were less evident. Agriculture remained dominant in the economic life, and farming methods continued to be much the same as those used in the past. Many enterprising young men emigrated to cities or to the West. After 1800, census takers sometimes found that the population in Kent and Sussex counties had actually decreased from the previous decade. The Anglican Church struggled to reestablish itself under the name of Protestant Episcopal, while the Methodists grew rapidly in membership. New villages appeared in Sussex County such as Laurel and Georgetown, and in Kent County, as at Milford. Except for the preparation of planks, shingles, and barrel staves, manufacturing continued to be only for local consumption.

The 1790s were a different age. The new nation, with its new Constitution and pride in its achievement in independence, looked forward with confidence to the future, as did the state with its new, more democratic constitution. Problems remained such as what to do about the exhausted soil, slavery, the lack of a public school system, and an inadequate transportation system, but there was a feeling among many of the inhabitants that hard work, thrift, and moral living would be rewarded in time—if not on this earth, in eternity.

XI ———————— AN EIGHTEENTH CENTURY POTPOURRI

DELAWARE IN 1789:
by Jedidiah Morse

Length: 92 miles Breadth: 16 miles
Between: 38°30′ and 40° North Latitude; 0° and 1° 45′ West Longitude.
Boundaries: Bounded north by the territorial line, which divides it from Pennsylvania; east by Delaware River and Bay; south, by a due east and west line, from Cape Henlopen, in lat. 38° 30′ to the middle of the peninsula, which line divides the state from Worcester County in Maryland; west, by Maryland, from which it is divided by a line drawn from the western termination of the southern boundary line, northwards up the said peninsula, till it touch or form a tangent to the western part of the periphery of the above mentioned territorial circle; containing about 1400 square miles.
Climate: In many parts unhealthy. The land is generally low and flat, which occasions the waters to stagnate, and the consequence is the inhabitants are subject to intermittents [fevers].
Civil Divisions. The Delaware state is divided into three counties, viz.

Counties	Chief Towns
Newcastle	Wilmington and Newcastle
Kent	Dover
Sussex	Milford and Lewistown

Rivers. Choptank, Nanticoke and Pocomoke, all have their sources in this state and are navigable for vessels of 50 or 60 tons, 20 or 30 miles into the country. They all run a westwardly course into Chesapeek [*sic*] Bay. The eastern side of the state, along Delaware Bay and River, is indented with a great number of small streams, but none considerable enough to merit a description.

Soil and Production. The south part of the state is a low flat country, and a considerable portion of it lies in forest. What is under cultivation is chiefly barren, except in Indian corn, of which it produces fine crops. In some places rye and flax may be raised, but wheat is foreigner in these parts. Where nature is deficient in one resource, she is generally bountiful in another. This is verified in the tall, thick forests of pines, which are manufactured into boards and exported in large quantities into every sea-port in the three adjoining states.

As you proceed north, the soil is more fertile and produces wheat in large quantities, which is the staple commodity of the state. They raise all the other kinds of grain common to Pennsylvania. The state has no mountain in it, except Thunder Hill, in the western part of Newcastle County, and generally level, except some small parts, which are stony and uneven.

Chief Towns. Dover, in the county of Kent, is the seat of government. It stands on Jones Creek, a few miles from the Delaware River, and consists of about 100 houses, principally of brick. Four streets intersect each other at right angles in the center of the town, whose incidencies form a spacious parade on the east side of which is an elegant state-house of brick. The town has a lively appearance and thrives on considerable trade with Philadelphia. Wheat is the principal article of export. The landing is five or six miles from the town of Dover.

Newcastle is 35 miles below Philadelphia, on the west bank of Delaware River. It was first settled by the Swedes, about the year, 1627, and called Stockholm. It was afterwards taken by the Dutch, and called New Amsterdam. When it fell into the hands of the English, it was called by its present name. It contains about 60 houses which have the aspect of decay, and was formerly the seat of government. This is the first town that was settled on Delaware River.

Wilmington is situated a mile and a half west of Delaware River, on Christiana Creek, 28 miles southward from Philadelphia. It is much the largest and pleasantest town in the state, containing about 100 houses, which are handsomely built upon a gentle ascent of an eminence, and show to great advantage as you sail up the Delaware.

Besides other public buildings, there is a flourishing academy of about 40 or 50 scholars, who are taught the languages, and some of the sciences by an able instructor. There is another academy at Newark in this county, which was incorporated in 1769, and then had 14 trustees.

Milford, the little emporium of Sussex county, is situated at the source of a small river, 15 miles from Delaware Bay, and 150 southward of Philadelphia. This town, which contains about 80 houses, has been built, except one house, since the Revolution. It is laid out with much taste, and is by no means disagreeable. The inhabitants are Episcopalians, Quakers and Methodists.

Duck Creek is 12 miles northwest from Dover, and has about 60 houses, which stand on one street. It carries on a considerable trade with Philadelphia—and certainly warrants a more pompous name. A mile south from this is situated Governor Collins' plantation. His house, which is large and elegant, stands a quarter of a mile from the road and has a pleasing effect upon the eye of the traveller.

Trade. The trade of this state, which is inconsiderable, is carried on principally with Philadelphia in boats and shallops.

The articles exported are principally wheat, corn, lumber and hay.

Religion. There are in this state 21 Presbyterian congregations belonging to the Synod of Philadelphia—seven Episcopal churches—six congregations of Baptists containing about 318 souls—four congregations of the people called Quakers; besides a Swedish church at Wilmington, which is one of the oldest churches in the United States, and a number of Methodists. *All* these denominations have free toleration by the constitution, and live together in harmony.

Population and Character. In the convention held at Philadelphia in the summer of 1787, the inhabitants of this state were reckoned at 37,000, which is about 26 for every square mile. There is no obvious characteristical difference between the inhabitants of this state and the Pennsylvanians.

(From Jedidiah Morse, "Delaware," in *The American Geography* [Elizabethtown, N.J., 1789], 345-349).

THE UNITED STATES GAZETTEER
by Joseph Scott

Delaware, state of, is situated between 38,29,30, and 39,51 N. lat. 0,2, E., and 0, 41, W. lon. It is bounded N. by Pennsylvania, E. by Delaware river, bay, and the Atlantic ocean, S. and W. by Maryland. Its greatest length, which is from N. to S. is 92 miles, and 33 in breadth from E. to W. but opposite the mouth of Red-Lion creek it is not more than 13 miles broad. It is divided into three counties, viz. New Castle, Kent and Sussex. Previous to the act of Union, which was passed at Chester, December 7th, 1682, for annexing to Pennsylvania, this state, then called the Territories, the counties of Kent and Sussex were called Jones' and Whorekill, or New Deal. It continued attached to Pennsylvania until the commencement of the late revolution, when it became a sovereign and independent state. The number of inhabitants

Map of Delaware ca. 1795.
Inscribed in pencil "Scott, 1795."
Courtesy of the Hagley Museum and Library.

according to the census of 1790 was 59,094, of whom 8,887 were slaves. This state in general may be considered as one extended plain, interspersed with few hills, but what lie in the N.W. W. parts of New Castle county; a single range, however, of these, stretches from N. to S. though not much elevated, through New Castle, Kent, and into the northern parts of Sussex county, parallel to Delaware river. This is the most elevated tract of land in the peninsula between the Chesapeak and Delaware bays. From a great number of swamps that lie contiguous to this ridge, flow the several rivers and creeks which water the peninsula. The most considerable of these beginning N. are Elk, Sassafras, Chester, Choptank and Nanticoke, which empty into the Chesapeak, and belong to the state of Maryland. In this state there are no streams so large as to merit the name of river, if we except Indian and St. Martin's in the southern parts of Sussex county, and either is inferior in point of extent and utility to Christiana and Brandywine creeks. The eastern side of the state along Delaware river, is indented with a great number of short creeks, which generally are bordered with extensive marshes, consequently have soft banks and muddy bottoms. A few only of these are navigable, on account of the numerous shoals with which they abound. There are few springs of water found here, but that deficiency is supplied by sinking wells, and many of the inhabitants think the water of these more salubrious than the limestone water of Pennsylvania; the latter often giving foreigners of a delicate constitution, and phlegmatic habit, a griping. This pernicious quality the well-water of Delaware does not possess.

But if many of the citizens of this state possess water which they think so excellent, and which to others, may appear an improbable circumstance in a country so level, and bordering on salt water; it is overbalanced by the evils arising from the great number of swamps & marshy ground which are met with. The noxious exhalations from these subjecting almost every foreigner, & many of the natives in autumn to an intertent fever.

Notwithstanding, many of the swamps bordering on the Delaware river, are rendered valuable by raising dykes or mounds of earth, to prevent the tides from overflowing them; when they yield large quantities of coarse hay. It has been already observed, that the northern and western parts of New Castle country are hilly; the height of these have been estimated at about 500 feet above the tide. Here the soil is generally clay, intermixed with gravel; but after passing Christiana creek, as you approach towards the Delaware river, the soil is a rich clay, intermixed with sand, and as you proceed to the southward it still becomes more so until you arrive in Sussex county, where it is chiefly a sandy soil. No state perhaps in the Union raises a larger proportion of good wheat than this. It is particularly sought for by the manufacturers of flour, and is thought to be little inferior to the genuine white wheat, which is raised in some counties on the Eastern shore of Maryland. Indian corn, barley, rye, buckwheat, flax, and potatoes, are not found of a better quality, or in greater abundance in any part of the Union. Apples, pears, peaches, cherries, plumbs [sic], and quinces grow here in great perfection, besides a great variety of small fruit.

The inhabitants manufacture a great part of their common wearing apparel. There are in the state 4 paper-mills, 3 rolling and slitting-mills; besides a greater number of merchant-mills for the manufacture of flour, than in any state of the Union, in proportion to its size. A manufactory of marine and glaubersalts, and magnesia has been lately established, a few miles below Lewis, on the sea-coast; and from the gentleman's practical knowledge of chymistry, his industry and perserverance, no doubt but it will become of considerable advantage, both to himself and the public at large—to the public, as it will in part contribute to render us independent of foreign nations, for some of those articles which our necessities demand; and until we in that respect become more independent than we are at present it is to be apprehended, we will not be respected in a manner correspondent to our feelings by some of those nations of Europe, to whom we are indebted for those supplies; for it is with nations as with men, he who can live independent of his neighbor will always be respected, more than the man whose necessities compel him to have recourse to his neighbour's abundance for supplies. There are few minerals discovered in this state; the only one that has yet been noticed, is bog iron ore, which is found among the branches of Nanticoke river, in Sussex county. Previous to the revolution, it was wrought to a large amount. It is of such a quality as to be peculiarly adapted to castings. The furnace is fallen to decay, but the forge still continues to manufacture a little. The staple commodities of this state are wheat and lumber, but the foreign trade is inconsiderable in proportion to the abundance of those articles which it furnishes; vast quantities being sent to Philadelphia, and shipped from that port. The exports in the year 1791 ending September 30th amounted to 199,840 dollars, in 1792—133,972 dollars, in 1793—71,242 dollars, and 1794 233,460 dollars. In the year 1791 this state owned and employed in the foreign trade, 7,813 tons of shipping, of these 4,610 were American. In the two subsequent years the tonnage was less, and last year it was more; always bearing a proportion to, and fluctuating with the exports. The militia of this state completes one division, which contains three brigades, each county being one, and each brigade contains three regiments. The most numerous religious denominations here are the Presbyterians, who have 24 churches, the Episcopalians 14, and the Baptists 7; there is besides these a considerable number of Methodists, particularly in the two lower counties.

New Castle County

New Castle, a populous and well cultivated county of the state of Delaware. It is 47 miles in length, and 20 in breadth, and contains 17,124 free inhabitants, and 2,562 slaves. Here are 2 snuff mills, 1 slitting-mill, 4 paper-mills, 60 for grinding grain and several fulling mills.

Chief towns: Wilmington and New Castle.

Christiana, a town of Delaware state; situated in New Castle County on a navigable creek of its own name. It contains about 50 dwellings and a Presbyterian church. The houses are chiefly of brick and stand on the ascent of a hill, which commands a fine prospect of the country towards Delaware River.

New Castle, a post-town of Delaware state, and the place where the courts of justice are held for New Castle county. It is situated on the W. side of Delaware River, 33 miles S.W. of Philadelphia. It contain about 70 dwellings, a court-house, jail; a Presbyterian and an Episcopalian church. This is the oldest town on Delaware River and was formerly the seat of government. Some years ago it was rather on the decline; but latterly it begins to flourish; and when the piers are built (for the erection of which a lottery has been established and drawn by permission of a law of that state), it will afford a safe retreat to vessels during the winter season—a circumstance that must add considerably to its prosperity.

Newport, a small post and trading town of the state of Delaware. It carries on a considerable trade with Philadelphia in flour. It contains about 30 houses.

Wilmington, a port of entry, and post town of the state of Delaware, and the most considerable and flourishing town in that state. It is situated in New Castle county, 2 miles W. of Delaware river; between Christiana and Brandywine creeks, the former of which admits vessels drawing 11 feet water. The creeks are here about one mile apart and uniting below the town, empty into the Delaware, at which place they are upwards of 300 yards wide. The town stands on the N. side of Christiana creek, upon the S. W. side of a hill, that rises 107 feet above the tide, on the N.E. side of the same hill, on Brandywine creek there are 13 mills & about 40 neat handsome dwellings. The town is regularly laid out, on a plan similar to Philadelphia, and contains upwards of 600 houses, mostly of brick. The houses for public worship are six, viz. two for Presbyterians, one for Swedish Episcopalians, one for Quakers, one for Baptists, and one for Methodists. The other public buildings are two market-houses, a poor-house, which stands on the W. side of the town, and is 120 feet by 40, and three stories high; and a large stone edifice, which was built designedly for an academy. It generally had from 40 to 50 scholars who were taught the dead languages, arithmetic, and the mathematics. The course of education was much interrupted during the late war, and the funds partly ruined by the depreciation of continental paper money. But by a late act of Congress, the institution is to be indemnified. Notwithstanding, the house has been lately purchased for the purpose of establishing a cotton manufactory, which is in considerable forwardness. A bolting cloth manufactory, and a distilary are the only manufactories established here, if we except those carried on by mechanics individually. This town carries on a very considerable trade with Philadelphia, and a brisk trade with foreign countries. It is said that Philadelphia receives every year on an average, from Christiana, and the other navigable creeks of Delaware, 265,000 barrels of flour, 300,000 bushels of wheat, 170,000 bushels of Indian corn, besides barley, oats, flax-seed, paper, slit-iron, snuff, slated provisions, & c. But this is not to be understood as the produce of the state of Delaware, for I apprehend it will be found, upon enquiry, that the largest proportion of the wheat and flour which passes through the Christiana to Philadelphia, is the produce of Chester, Lancaster, York, Dauphin, and Cumberland counties in Pennsylvania. It is said that upwards of 500,000 dollars worth of flour are manufactured on the Christiana, within two or three miles of the navigation. The exports to foreign countries in the year ending September 30th, 1794, amounted to 233,461 dollars. About the year 1735, the first houses were built here, and the town a few years afterwards was incorporated, and is governed by two burgesses, six assistants, and two constables; all of whom are elected annually.

The mills on Brandywine, as we have mentioned already, are thirteen; these are, no doubt, the most valuable collection of mills in the United States, or perhaps in any other country, Twelve of them are merchant mills, and one a saw mill. They are scarcely half a mile from Wilmington. There are about 300,000 bushels of wheat and corn ground here annually; but it is supposed that if they were constantly supplied with grain, they would grind 400,000. They give employment to about 200 persons, viz. 40 to attend the mills, from 50 to 70 coopers, to make casks for the flour, beside those employed in the transportation of wheat and flour, and the rest in various other occupations connected with the mills.

The navigation is so convenient that a sloop carrying 1,000 bushels will lay along side of any of the mills to load, or unload; besides some of them will admit vessels of 2,000 bushels burthen. The vessels are unloaded with singular expedition, owing to the machines introduced by the ingenious Mr. Oliver Evans, who has lately published a valuable Work, entitled the Young Mill-Wright's Guide. There have been frequent instances of 1,000 bushels being carried to the height of four stories in four hours. By means of Mr. Evans' machinery, the wheat will be received on the shallops' deck, thence carried to the upper loft of the mill, and a large quantity of the same returned in flour, on the floor, ready for packing, without the assistance of manual labour, but in a very small degree. It is about 40 years since the first mill was built here. A stone bridge has been erected over the creek, at this place from which the mills, the dwellings, and the vessels loading and unloading, present an agreeable appearance.

Kent County

Kent, a rich, populous and fertile county of the state of Delaware. It contains 16,620 free inhabitants and 2,300 slaves. The lands in this county are esteemed the richest in the state.

It well watered by several small streams that empty into the Delaware. Chief town: Dover.

Dover, the metropolis of the state of Delaware, situated in Kent County, on Jones Creek, 4 miles direct from Delaware River, and 76 S.S.W. of Philadelphia. It consists of four streets which intersect each other at right angles. The area included within these intersections forms a handsome and spacious parade. On the east side of the parade is an elegant statehouse of brick, which gives an air of grandeur to the town. The dwellings, which are about 120, are chiefly of brick. It carries on a brisk trade with Philadelphia, chiefly in wheat, but the landing is five miles from town.

Duck Creek Cross Roads, or Salisbury, a considerable and flourishing town of the state of Delaware, situated on Duck Creek, which partly separates Kent and New Castle Counties. It consists of one street on which are erected about 90 dwellings. It carries on a brisk trade with Philadelphia and is one of the best wheat-markets in the state.

Frederica, a post-town of the state of Delaware, situated in Kent County on the W. side of a branch of Motherkill Creek, 7 miles N. of Milford. It contains between 30 and 40 houses.

Milford, a post town of the state of Delaware, agreeably situated on the N. side of Muspilion Creek. It contains nearly 100 houses, which were all built since the war, except one. The inhabitants are Methodists, Espiscopalians and Quakers.

Sussex County

Sussex, a large maritime county of the state of Delaware, containing 16,483 free persons, and 4,025 slaves. It is 44 miles in length and 43 in breadth. The lands in this county are generally low, sandy and poor. Chief town: Georgetown.

Daggsbury, a post-town of the state of Delaware, situated in Sussex County, on the N. side of Pepers Creek, which empties into Indian River. It contains about 40 houses.

Georgetown, the chief town of Sussex County, situated near the center of the county. It contains 30 houses and was lately made the seat of justice.

Lewistown, formerly the chief town of Sussex county, but the courts of justice have been lately removed to Georgetown. It is pleasantly situated on Lewis Creek, 3 miles above its conflux with Delaware Bay, and the same distance W. by N. of the light-house on Cape Henlopen. It contains 100 dwellings, a Presbyterian and Methodist church, a courthouse and jail. The situation of the town is upon a gentle eminence, commanding a view of the light-house, bay and ocean. The creek does not admit large vessels up to the town, having only 6 feet water, but that deficiency might be easily removed by cutting a canal from Rehoboth bay, which is but a short distance, and all the way a marsh, except three quarters of a mile. Previous to the late revolution, a bridge, and causeway, of considerable extent were erected over the creek, and marsh leading to the cape and light-house. As they were just completed, the British ships of war came into the road of Lewis. In order therefore to obstruct the communication, it was thought prudent to remove part of the work; being afterwards neglected, it was wholly in ruins at the end of the year. A bridge has lately been finished on the same plan, but on a new foundation, at the expence of individuals. It extends nearly a quarter of a mile from the town towards the beach, over a wide creek and marsh which open an easy and convenient communication with the cape.

On Cape-Henlopen, a lighthouse has been erected since the war; the former one being burnt in 1777. It is a handsome stone structure in the form of an octogan and 115 feet high and stands upon ground elevated: nearly the same height above the level of the seat. The lantern is between 7 and 8 feet square, lighted with 8 lamps; around the lantern, at a little distance, is a strong wire network, in order to prevent birds from breaking the glass at night. Yet strange as it may appear, upwards of 110 birds of different kinds were found dead one morning shortly after it was erected, and one duck, in particular, flew against it with such force, as to break through both wire and glass, and was found dead in the lantern next morning. But latterly there are few accidents happen. How it is that the birds are becoming more sensible of their danger is a question perhaps worthy the attention of the naturalist, as we cannot suppose any of those that flew against the lantern ever returned to communicate the danger to their kind. The yearly expense of the light-house is estimated at £650.

(Joseph Scott, *The United States Gazetteer,* Philadelphia, 1795)

For the Delaware Gazette
O D E,
For the Anniversary of American INDEPENDENCE,
July 5, 1789.
Jam redit et virgo, redeunt saturnia regna:
Jam nova progenies coelo demittitur alto.

Virg.

The day returns, well known to fame,
Columbia's sons the dawn proclaim,
    And greet th' auspicious morn!
Loud cannons shake the concave sky,
The hills, the vales, the woods reply—
    "A mighty empire born!"

Thirteen long years have roll'd away,
Since freedom marked this brilliant day,
    And snap'd a despot's chain;
Columbia's (a) seers, with one accord,
Fearless pronounced the (b) final word,
    That split a world in twain!

Thro' seas of gore, with horror fraught,
Her sons with dauntless valor fought,
    The doubtful strife withstood!
Eight years of war, with crimson stain,
Polluted ev'ry grove and plain,
    And rivers swell'd with blood.

The scene is past!—sweet peace returns!
No more a wasted country mourns
    Her ruin'd fields and towns:
In social circles now we meet,
The great event, well pleas'd, to greet,
    While harmless mirth abounds.

Gladness each countenance illumes,
Magnolia's waft their rich perfumes
    In honor to the day!
The birds in loftier numbers sing,—
E'en summer smiles like rosy spring,
    Enraptur'd with the lay.

For every state Columbia claims,
A year old (c) Saturn fondly names,
    And hails them free for ever:
If harmony their councils sway,
No force shall bring them to decay,
    No power shall e'er dessever.

To the fair banks of (d) Ion, in form we repair,
For friendship attends us, and pleasure dwells here,
While (e) Ceres and (f) Bacchus unitedly reign,
And joy undissembled, enlivens the plain:
But from our pastimes be banished the man,
Who faction and strife, would ingratefully plant.

Astrea (g) came down with a scroll in her hand,
For Washington seal'd and directed:
"This parchment," she cried "is the law of your land
By this shall your states be protected."

"Twas form'd and devised in the synod of Jove,
    While (h) Pallas directed the pen:
In haste I was sent from the councils above,
    To publish the tidings to men."

"All hail!" cried the patriot, "the boom I receive,
    Blest gift from their godheads on high!
Its lore from confusion our land shall retrieve,
    Its laws shall all faction defy."

"Thrice happy my country!—to which it is given,
    With justice and glory to rise!
Regarded with love—by the regents of heaven,
    Chief fav'rite and joy of the skies!"

Then soon in her archives these laws were recorded,
   Columbia approved of the same:
Their happy design every blessing afforded,
   Then gave the bright schedule to fame.

Soon fame did her work, and the tidings were spread,
From countries far east, to the southward they sped:—
From Atlas' bleak shores she extended her voice,
And the mountains in unison, echo'd—"rejoice."

Columbia began, " 'Tis my will O my son!
   (The gods of the choice all approve,)
With wisdom to rule the great empire you won,
   In harmony, justice and love."

"I come at the call," cried the hero ador'd,
   ("Tho' reluctant I leave my fair seat,")
In peace now to sway what was gain'd by the sword,
   Far, far from (i) Mount Vernon's retreat.

O'er a world of brave freeman,—how glorious to reign
Whose honor and courage have known not a stain:
Whose souls all united approve with one breath,
The man, who rescu'd them from slavery and death.

To heroes now, who moulder in the grave,
Who gave their lives this chosen land to save:
Oh! to their much-lov'd memory drop the tear,
And honor those, who once was held so dear.

Haslet (j) tho' born on far Ierne's shore,
At Princeton falls,—besmear'd with human gore.
Holland (k),—brave leader of some chosen (l) choirs
Flush in the Van, at Germantown expires.
(m) Adams and Stephens, both Columbian sons,
Sink 'mid the slaughter of a despot's guns.

The willing muse, would fain the tribute pay,
But Phoebus chides th' bold, th' unequal lay.
Forgive, lov'd shades,—if no funeral verse,
Extol your merits, or adorn your herse!
Some skillful bard of real poetic name,
Shall write them glorious on the roll of fame.

J***P****

Dover, July

(a) Continental Congress
(b) Declaration of Independence 1776
(c) The God of time, represented with a scythe in his right hand, and a hour-glass in his left.
(d) Ion, or Ionia; Dover river, poetically so called.
(e) (f) Figuratively put, for good eat and drinking.
(g) The Goddess of justice, who resided in the world during the golden age of Saturn: but when the iron age, under Jupiter commenced, she fled from heaven, leaving the earth deluged with human blood.—Vide Ovid Met. In the year 1775 she took a second flight:—but it is to be hoped she will again return, and dwell among us, under the happy auspices of the Federal Government, and the wise administration of our illustrious President.
(h) Minerva, or Pallas, the Goddess of wisdom and of war.
(i) The elegant country seat, of our worthy President-General.
(j) John Haslet, esq, was born in Ireland and educated for a dissenting clergyman,—but relinquishing that calling, he apply'd himself with success to the Study of Physic, which he practised many years in Kent county on Delaware, with profit and reputation. He was frequently chosen a representative in the general assembly, for that country, where his talents as a statesman, an orator, and an author; were equally admired.—And finally was appointed colonel commandant of the regular troops of Delaware: The circumstances of his glorious death are too recent, and well-known to require a particular description at this time.
(k) Captain Thomas Holland, was a native of England, and had formerly been in that service.
(l) Choirs, by poetical license, for Corps.
(m) Captain Nathan Adams and James Stephens, natives of Kent county. The above gentlemen were all officers under the command of colonel Haslet: and were also slain during the war.

Delaware Gazette, August 8, 1789.

CELEBRATION OF THE FOURTH OF JULY IN DOVER IN 1793

By Thomas Rodney

This being the anniversary of Independence, I went to Dover merily as a spectator. I light at Captn. Wilsons and did not leave the House. There was a company of twenty or thirty that had appointed to celebrate the day, to wit, Doctr. Miller,

Doctr. Sykes, and others. In composing the toasts it was
proposed that Genl. Washington should be given, but this, it
seems, was strenuously opposed by Doctr. Miller, who said
he was not more than another man, and moved that equality
should be given as a toast, which was opposed by Doctr.
Sykes, and Bob Clark swore he wold not drink any toast
that savoured the least of the French convention, so that
much warm dispute arose in composing the toasts, as the
report reached us. They had two pieces of cannon, and the
firing was to be conducted by Captn. M. McCall, and they
were to supply him in the usual way with a copy of the
toasts, but did not. After firing twice, he called for a copy of
the toast, but they would not send any. Whereupon he became very outrageous, swore he would fire no more and
immediately ordered the guns down the street. The Club
seeing this, broke up and left the court house where they were
drinking and followed and seized McCall and the guns. J.
Millis, Charles Hylliard and Joseph Miller were the persons
who seized McCall on this occasion. Rees at first opposed
and then joined them. Whereupon a scuffle ensued, but the
rejoiners being strongest, carried off the guns to the court
house, where McCalls men (for he had left them) made
another scuffle, but one of them (William Peirce) being sent
to goal by the Chief Justice, the firing then went on, conducted by Wm. Rees, but McCall being very angry afterward, went up and encurraged one of his men (Coleman) to
set upon Rees and being a stout fellow, he beat Rees. This had
like to have brot. on a general scuffle, but it blew over, and
McCall upon the whole incurred a defeat. After the firing
was over, Bob Clark, though an errant coward himself, and
after hearing McCall was gone home, abused him very much,
that is with calling him by every approbius name, &c. This
was the first instance of the day, being clouded by an distur-
bance in Dover of this sort, but there was a strong spirit of
French party & Brittish Party at the bottom, as appeared by
the disputes that arose about the toasts, &c.

T[homas]. R[odney].

I saw & heard as a cool spectator without emotion, being determined not to meddle, but where great & good occasion requires to aid the welfare of my country.
(Thomas Rodney Collection, Box 10, Historical Society of Delaware.)

THE ROLE OF WOMEN
AN ORATION

(Pronounced on the 5th July, 1790, by James Tilton, M.D., President of the Delaware State Society of the Cincinnati)

EXTRACT

As a member of the Cincinnati, I feel myself under double obligation to pay due respect to the fair sex. When our society was attacked by designing men, and even weak brethren were drawn into unworthy suspicions of our association, we every where found countenance and protection from the ladies. Their benevolent hearts rejected the ungrateful idea that men foremost in danger and exertions for delivering their country from tyranny should be the first to mar the fair plot of equal liberty. It was inexplicable, indeed, to the more candid and impartial sex, how a few associators, without a single legal advantage should assume to themselves high prerogative and distinction. Envious men may indeed fear and persecute the society, as they did Aristides of old, for their superior virtues; but the justice of our country women has universally decreed that our profession is fair and honorable, and the means employed perfectly justifiable.

But a sense of gratitude is not the only motive that engages me to support the rank and importance of the fair sex. The resolution I have taken to give *incessant attention to preserve inviolate the sacred rights of human nature,* lays me under the strongest obligation to advocate the just equality in political society. The men may boast of the strength of arm and superior authority; the women, under the modest term of influence, are of equal importance. The men possess the more ostensible powers of making and executing the laws; the women in every free country have an absolute control of manners: and it is confessed, that in a republic manners are of equal importance with laws. I should therefore be uncandid, did I not on this occasion declare that for the manners of our country, our fair patriots are solely responsible.

From the most savage to the most enlightened people, the female parent is considered of greatest importance to the defendants, by stamping their manners and sentiments in the early period of childhood and youth. An American Indian always quotes his mother, for his polite and respectful manners, and if we fail in the least of that formal respect required by the yellow Sachem, he immediately reproaches our mothers. *Cyrus, Scipio,* and *Washington* acknowledge in pious gratitude to their female parents that the foundation of their fame was laid in the wise instructions of maternal education. All authority agrees in establishing the native influence and important duty of the mother,

"To teach the young idea how to shoot." [i.e., grow]

And you, my younger and fairest sisters, will be duly guarded against those seducing triflers, who tell you it is no matter what a woman says or does. Believe me rather, your very thoughts and opinions are of the utmost consequence to the public. You possess the mighty powers of metamorphosing the silken beau into a rational man, content and pleased with a home spun dress, and ambitious of plain and artless manners. Were it possible for you to lavish your smiles, especially upon frivolous coxcombs, the fascinating influence might be such, as to degrade our youth into a mean obsequiousness, that might lead them even to forget their liberty, and aptly fit them to become the servants of servants. But I indulge a more pleasing prospect, when our young and rising heroes shall be prompted to exertions the most liberal, generous and brave, in confident expectation that their successful endeavors shall be crowned by your nobler charms, as the prize of virtue and honor.

Were it right or necessary on this occasion to reason from any other motive than the love of country, I might adduce the history of the world to shew that from remotest India to Europe and America, women are respectable and happy in exact proportion to the liberty and civilization of their country. It would give you pain to rehearse the mean and subordinate condition of the women in Asiatic countries. Neither would a recital of the Chesterfieldian manners of Europe, where women are treated as mere engines in the hands of designing and interested men, please my fair audience. But it is with pleasure I acknowledge their native equality and dwell upon the fair prospect of perfecting the female character in this, our country. Here no austere religon shackles the mind; no tyrannic arm dare oppress the weaker sex. Their talents and their virtues have free course; *they may run and be glorified.* Science and true philosphy begin already to embellish domestic economy, and we enjoy the near prospect, when female benevolence, candor and justice shall extend their benign influence, to the heightening of every improvement in political society.

It requires no superstition, indeed, to view with an eye of piety the designs of Providence, in that accumulation of powerful motives, by which our fair patriots are animated to the most splendid attainments. For in America, it may be emphatically said that the honor of your *God*—the love of your country—the glory of your descendants—your own fame and interest in the world, all conspire to engage you to *reverence yourselves.*

But the time and the occasion, my fair hearers, will not permit me to exhaust this important subject—Your own reflections must fill up the necessary comments—remembering that from *Adam* to this day, men never could be virtuous alone; that our enlightened clergy may preach in vain; in vain will our ablest senators legislate; even the vows of the Cincinnati shall prove weak and fruitless, without your cordial concurrence in the spirit of patriotism.

An animated orator, my fellow citizens, might entertain

you till evening, with a succession of thoughts most worthy of your attention. My slender stock is nearly exhausted. Indulge me, however, before I conclude, in a reflection or two, equally applicable to men, women and children.

When we compare the growing light and liberty of our country with that of any other that does or ever did exist; when we reflect upon the probable growth of our empire in extent, happiness and fame; when rooted and grounded, as we ought to be in *Spartan* attachment to our native land; how natural is it for us to contemplate our *Delaware* as another *Eurotas!* to love the beautiful little state we live in, as another Lacedaemon! to regard *America,* as more favored of heaven, more glorious among men than a former *Greece!*

(*Delaware Gazette,* July 10, 1790.)

JOHN THELWELL: SCHOOLMASTER

But we must not pass this primitive place of worship [the Methodist meeting house] without a tribute of respect to John Thelwell, its devoted patron from its early dawn, and faithful until death. "The Lord shall count, when he writeth up the people, that this man was born there." It would be easier for us to say what he did not than to recount his numerous duties. He was a ruler, an exhorter, and an efficient class-leader with these people. He was clerk of the markets, too, and once he weighed a woman's butter which was wanting in balance, and was about to take away the basket. She being keen-sighted, and he having but one eye, she took the advantage by daubing a pound in the other eye, and thus made off with her effects.

He held the office of bell-man from time immemorial, as crier. Many at this day remember Daddy Thelwell and his big bell, tingling as he passed, and warning the burgesses to attend their meeting in the little town chamber over the end of the lower market-house. Also for sales of property and goods at auction. Those are yet living who heard the joyful sound of his old bell ringing in their ears, arousing them from repose, his voice echoing loud and long, "Cornwallis is taken! Cornwallis is taken!"

Could you believe, after being faithful to all these duties, he should be a schoolmaster, and of some note, too!

The more ancient Horn Book scarcely now remembered, became out of use in this country, and ceased to be imported from England, when we undertook to teach ourselves learning after the Revolution. It was soon below our expectations, for it only contained the alphabetic letters, the numerals, and the Lord's prayer. These, fastened on a small thin board, about the size of a small spelling-book page, were securely nailed to it with a strip of bright brass for a margin, and covered with a plate of horn so transparent as to render the text clearly to be read, yet fully defended from the unwashed fingers of the pupils. . . .

But the intruding successor to teach the alphabet—spelling, reading and grammar—was Dilworth's spelling-book, with small print, like old worn-out newspaper type. This generation would not bend their minds to study such dim lights. Most boys and girls here were his pupils, at least during part of their school days.

At the foot of Quaker Hill, Mr. Thelwell had commenced teaching, but was soon promoted to the little Senate Chamber over the market-house, and this, at the corner of Third and King Streets, was long his room. The boys' entrance was front, the girls' up an alley. Even in those *primitive* days, there were some unruly children; but he adhered most strictly to the letter of Solomon's advice, and "never spared the rod." The rattan or ferule seemed to be in perpetual motion, and were as common in his seminary as gymnastics are at this day, and woe to the boy mouted to receive the reward of his exploits or omissions! But wondrous strange if after such an exhibition he should return to school subdued. It can only be accounted for, that Independence was not fully understood in the young Republic. Certainly it was not carried out as in this day.

The Bible was used for the senior class, and also Gough's Arithmetic, with sums in simple division that would fill a large slate, and puzzle many a brain, and cause showers of tears. This school was opened every morning by prayer and singing a hymn.

The village all declared how much he knew;
'Twas certain he could write and cipher too;
Lands he could measure, terms and tides presage,
And e'en the story ran that he could gauge.
But past is all his fame. The very spot
Where many a time he triumphed is forgot.

Miss Debby Thelwell, the eldest daughter, assisted and kept the girls in order; she was a very worthy woman, but with no literary pretensions. Miss Polly rarely entered; she was timid and more refined. After the father's death, the sisters united, and taught young children for many years. In old age, this worthy family were removed by death from useful employment, having contributed their share of good to this community.

(Elizabeth Montgomery, *Reminiscences of Wilmington* [Wilmington, 1851], 227-229.)

SCHOOLS IN WILMINGTON IN THE 1780s

The state of schools in Wilmington, "sixty years ago," has before been alluded to. It is well known to many yet living [in 1846] that, in country places, it was then common to employ as schoolmaster, any tolerably decent looking traveller would apply for office. The first and most important inquiry was at how low a price would he teach a child for three calendar months. If that question was satisfactorily settled, and it was found that he could "read, write and cypher,'' the bargain was concluded. It most frequently happened that the applicant was a foreigner, who spoke English (if it can be said that he spoke it at all) with a broad, uncouth accent or vile brogue; announcing that he had just come ashore from some passenger ship; and it very often turned out that he was a habitual drunkard, who spent a goodly portion of his time during school hours in sleep. To such teachers was it then common to expose the morals of children!

In Wilmington, however, even "sixty years ago," things were not quite so bad. The teachers were frequently good moral characters, though often very deficient in other respects. The course of instruction very rarely extended beyond reading, writing and arithmetic. About the year 1787, the committee having the charge of the school "on the hill," procured a teacher from Philadelphia, who was at that time accounted an extraordinary scholar, as he could teach Latin and Greek. He introduced, as an additional branch of instruction, English grammar; but for want of suitable books for the purpose, his effort was almost an entire failure. No other branches were attempted. Geography was no more thought of as a branch of school education than Astrology.

As late as the time we are now alluding to, the old barbarous custom of "barring out" had not become entirely obsolete. The last attempt of the kind was so disastrous that it never was repeated in that house. It took place during the incumbency of the late John Webster, a man of considerable notoriety afterwards in Wilmington. On the evening before Christmas, the boys had got possession of the school-house, and employed themselves in carrying a quantity of wood from the cellar, and piling it against the doors inside of the room. They then secured all the windows but one, which was kept open as a kind of drawbridge to go into the castle.

Next morning early, such of the boys as had courage to stand a siege, entered the fortress, and fastening the place of entry, awaited with anxiety the arrival of the master. At length he made his appearance, and after unlocking the door as usual, he found it would not turn upon its hinges. On

searching after the cause, he discovered that the house was in
possession of his scholards who had barred every entrance,
and now refused him admission, unless, on his honor, he
would promise them a vacation for the day. To this humbling
condition he refused to submit; and now came on the tug of
war.

After some fruitless attempts to open a breach in the
ramparts, and while the master was looking for more effectual means to gain the fort, some elderly Friends were discovered coming up the hill, with deliberate step, on their way
to meeting; for this memorable siege happened on their day
for public worship. No sooner had they understood the case,
than they promptly joined the assailing force. One of them
procured a crow-bar, and, with a crash that made every
defender of the place to tremble, bursted open a window,
fronting on West Street. Many of the besieged, and especially the weaker members of the garrison, now saw that all
chance of escape was lost. But some of the larger boys, who
foresaw that they would have to bear the heaviest part of the
consequences, made an effort to get away; and opening a
window on the back part of the house, began to jump out; but
one of the assailants not feeling easy that the guiltiest should
so avoid the salutary inflictions which awaited them, had
seasonably stationed himself at the place of sortie, and with
his cane so effectually administered the law of Moses, which
forbids that the guilty should go free, that the greater part
surrendered at discretion. A regular court for the trial of the
offenders was now held, in the presence of the grave captors,
who sat as judges in the case, the schoolmaster being the
executive officer; and such was the efficancy of their administration, that the stoutest heart ever afterwards quailed at the
bare suggestion of a "barring out."

(From Benjamin Ferris, *A History of the Original Settlements
on the Delaware* [Wilmington, 1846], 285-287.)

THE SCHOOL DAYS OF JOHN HAMILTON OF WILMINGTON

I think my memory can bear me as far back as (A.D.) One thousand seven hundred and eighty five, at least, in which year I commenced my school career with a very worthy scientific man of the name of [John] Filson, who had previously been employed in surveying the lands of Kentucky, then a wilderness, and of which he published a map. He did not remain long in Wilmington before he returned again to the Western Wilds, and at length fell beneath an Indians tomahawk, when on a surveying excursion.

My next pedagogue was a gentleman [probably Joseph Anderson, who became a judge and U.S. Senator from Tennessee] who has occupied a distinguished and elevated situation in public life. While he taught his little school, he, at the same time, devoted all his leisure time to the study of the law, under the late worthy and much regretted Judge Bedford. That object accomplished, he dismissed his scholars, and shaped his course West in quest of adventures. . . .

What Wilmington does not remember, or, if too young to recollect, has not heard of Old Master John Thelwell, who "taught the young ideas how to shoot," during the space of at least half a century. He was the complete Dicky Gossip of the Town, filling, I cannot now enumerate, how many of the offices, civil, military and ecclesiastical. In the execution of the duties of one of them (Clerk of the Market), he was rather too rigid (being entitled I believe to one half of the spoil). How often have I stood by and almost, with tears in my eyes in sympathy with those flowing from a poor female, deprived of her whole adventure of butter, because it was found a little wanting—an adventure on which she had perhaps already drawn in anticipation, for at least two thirds, on some neighboring store, for holiday and Sunday finery. It was Master Thelwell's misfortune to be dark of one eye (although the other appeared amply adequate to sweep a compass around the Horizon, and embrace every object within its vision, particularly in the Market). A tradition ran among the boys, I know not with what foundation, that this misfortune proceeded from a light pound of butter, discharged in his face, while making a haul one day.

It would be rather a tedious job to attempt to enumerate and particularize all the offices and places filled by this gentleman. One important station I well remember was Marshall at all funerals, and no one in the town could be marched to their long home without being escorted by him, and followed by all his urchin pupils. When the Methodistical fever reached our little town, he was one of the first to imbibe the infection, and was file leader, there, performing always the duties of clerk, or raiser of the hymns—and, sometimes, in a dernier resort, attempted to eschaet a little. I could say more of poor Old Master Thelwell, but will sum up all in announcing him to have been a very worthy, good sort of man. Peace to his Manes, he has been many years since gathered to his fathers, after having educated (or at least imparted the rudiments) to at least three generations of Wilmingtonians.

Let me See! —I then enlisted in the ranks of a plain Friend, called Solomon Fussell, and as strict a disciplinarian as ever I served under. His left hand had been taken off by the wrist— How, I know not, but presume not in War— which admirably served him to lift a boys leg, while, with the right hand, he plied his birch lustily "a posteriori." At that time we generally wore leather breeches, the punishment may therefore be readily conceived.

Before the ninth winter had passed over my head, I was removed to the Latin School in the Wilmington Academy, at the time, under the care of Mr. William (afterwards Rev.) Maffit. The institution was then well filled with pupils, many of whom have since made some figure in public life; and a far greater proportion gone to their long homes. Mr. W. Maffit, on taking Holy Orders, was succeeded by his brother John (a real Boatswain's Mate in inflicting punishment), under the stimulus of whose goad I floundered along as through an unturnpiked road at the breaking up of frost in the spring, until I had attained my fourteenth years, when, having become proficient in Latin and Greek, it was deemed necessary I should have to read and write English. For at those classical schools, the professors and teachers do not consider these of any importance whatever.

(From John Hamilton, "Some Reminiscences of Wilm't'n and My Youthful Days &c., &c.," *Delaware History*, 1[1946]: 89-91.)

THE SCHOOL DAYS OF WILLIAM MORGAN (1780–1857) IN SUSSEX COUNTY

I was sent to school in my sixth year, had to go about a mile and a half in winter, as there ware no summer schools at that time in the neighbourhood. The home the school was kept in was pine slabs, notched up, and covered with boards and slabs, a hole cut at the top of the roof at one end to let out the smoke. The fire being made on the ground, with a back of bricks and clay, three or four feet high to keep the fire from burning the house.

As to windows, we could do very well without any, for we could see through the craks between the slabs and have as much air as we wanted. All the school books that I have any recolection of was Dilworth's spelling book and arithmatic with the bible and testament.

The school master whoes name was Thomas Gray was considered to be a greate schollar. He used to teach us to pronounce would, "wold," could, "cold," "warmet," for walnut, "ponger," for porringer, &c., &c. In this way I first began the rudiments of the english language. I presume I made as greate progress as any other child of my oppertunity, but may sure it was no greate things. Three months ended the school for that term, and no more until next winter. By this time I had forgotten what I had learned.

The second winter i progressed so far as to be able to read the easy lessons in Dilworth's spelling book. About this time my father boughte me a small book, an extract from Gold-smith's animated nature. This book I was wonderfully taken up with and persued it (for the pictures sake) and so much that my father made me quit it, as he said it took up to much of my time. This went hard with me, as I was very intent to know and learn the nature of things.

There were no more schools in the neighbourhood for two or three years after this. At length the neighbours employed an old lady by the name of Isabella Gladson to teach school at an old logged house, very little better than the slabbed one, only it was built in the woods and was some warmer in winter and plenty of lizards, scorpions and snakes about it in summer time.

The manner of teaching was: First the spelling book, then the new testament, then the bible, then to write from copy plates. After going five or six months in the course of two or three years, I learend to read the Testiment and Bible and to write joining hand, as it was called.

I have ever been thankful that I went to school where I was lerned to read the Scriptures. It has proved a greate source of comfort and satisfaction to me from that day to this. To me it has always appeared to be a shame and scandal to the Christian name to banish the Scriptures from schools, as it is from most schools at this day in this country.

In my sixteenth year I went about two miles to school two and a half months in winter. I had to cross a rappid branch in a conoe, and to follow the course of the branch about a quarter of a mile before I could land. This I had to do morning and evening, and was frequently in danger of being drowned. At this school I learend writing and arithmatic as far as the single rule of three. This was the last school I ever went to as a lerner. It may be observed that I went some years before this to some ephemera schools, but this was all I lerned any thing at of consequence.

(From Harold Hancock, "William Morgan's Autobiography and Diary: Life in Sussex County, 1780-1857," *Delaware History*, 19 [1980], 42-43. The original autobiography and diary are in the Delaware State Archives.)

ON THE EDUCATION OF YOUTH: AN ESSAY
HUMBLY OFFERED TO THE CONSIDERATION
OF PARENTS

by Thomas Dilworth

The right education of children is a thing of the highest importance, both to themselves and to the commonwealth. It is this which is the natural means of preserving religion and virtue in the world; and the earlier *good instructions* are given, the more lasting will be their impression. For it is as unnatural to deny *these* to children, as it would be to withhold from them their necessary subsistance. And happy are those, that by a religious *education* and watchful care of their *parents,* their wise *precepts* and good *examples,* have contracted such a love of virtue and hatred of vice, as to be removed out of the way of temptations. And 'tis owing to the want of education, that many, when they leave their schools, do not prove so well qualified as might be expected. This great *omission* being, for the most part, chargeable on the *parents,* I hope the following particulars, which are the common voice of our profession, will not be taken amiss. And,

1. A constant attendance at *school* is one main axis whereon the great wheel of *education* turns. Therefore, if that observation, which is commonly made by parents be true, *that the masters have holidays enough of their own making,* there is, by their own confession, no necessity for them to make an addition.

2. Parents should never let their own commands run counter to their master's, but whatever task he imposes on his pupils,

to be done at home, they should be careful to have it performed in the best manner, in order to keep them out of idlesness. *"For vacant hours move too heavily and rust and filth along with them; and 'tis full employment and a close application to business that is the only barrier to keep out the enemy and save the future man."* (Watt's *Essay*)

3. Parents themselves should endeavour to be sensible of their children's *defects* and want of *parts,* and not blame the master for neglect when his greatest skill with some will produce but a small share of improvement. But the greatest misfortune is as the proverb expressed it: *Every bird thinks her own young the fairest:* and the tender *mother,* tho' her son be of an ungovernable temper will not scruple to say, *He is a meek child, and will do more with a word than a blow,* when neither *words* nor *blow* are available. On the other hand, some children are of a very dull and heavy disposition, and are a long time in gathering but little learning; and yet their parents think them as capable of *instruction,* as those who have the most bright and prominent parts: And when it happens that they improve but slowly, though it be in proportion to their own abilities, they are hurried about from school to school, till at last they lose that share of learning, which otherwise, by staying at the same school they have might have been masters of. Just like a *sick* but *impatient* man, who employs a physician to cure him of his *malady,* because the distemper requires *time* as well as skill to procure his health tells him "He has all along take a *wrong* method," turns him off, and then applies to another, whom he serves in the same manner; and so proceeds till the *distemper* proves incurable.

4. It is highly necessary that children should be early made sensible of the scandal of telling a *lye:* To this end, parents must inculcate upon them, betimes, that most necessary virtue of speaking the truth as one of the best and strongest bonds of *human society* and *commerce* and the foundation of all *moral honesty.*

5. *Injustice* (I mean the tricking each other in trifles, which so frequently happens among children, and is often counte-

nanced by the parents and looked on as a sign of very *promising genius*), ought to be discouraged betimes; lest it should betray them into the vile sin of *pilfering* or *purloining* in their riper years; to which the grand enemy of mankind is not wanting to prompt them by his suggestions whenever he finds their inclinations have a tendency that way.

6. *Immoderate anger* and desire of *revenge* must never be suffered to take root in children. For (as a most reverend divine, A. B. Tillotson, observes), *"If any of these be cherished, or even let alone in them, they will in a short time grow headstrong and unruly: And when they come to be men, will corrupt the judgment, turn good nature into ill humour, and understanding into prejudice and wilfulness."*

7. Children are very apt to say at home what they see and hear at school, and oftentimes more than is true, and some parents, as often, are weak enough to believe it. Hence arise those great uneasinesses between the *parents* and the *master,* which sometimes are carried so high, as for the parent, in the presence of the child, to reproach him with hard names, and perhaps with more abusive language.

8. The last things that I shall take notice of is that while the master endeavours to keep *peace,* good *harmony,* and *friendship* among his scholars, they are generally taught the reverse at home. "It is indeed but too common for children to encourage one another and be encouraged by their friends in that savage and brutal way of contention, and to count it as a hopeful sign of mettle in them to give the last *blow,* if not the *first,* whenever they are provoked; forgetting at the same time, that to teach children betimes to love and be good natured to others, is to lay early the true foundation of an *honest man.* Add to this, that cruel delight which some are seen to take in tormenting and worrying such poor *animals* and *insects* as have the misfortune to fall into their hands. "But children should not only be restrained from such *barbarous diversions,* but should be bred up from the beginning to an abhorrence of them," [Talbot's *Christian Schoolmaster*], and at the same time be taught that great rule of humanity, *to do to others as we would they should do to us.*

From what has been said relating to the management of children *at home,* the necessity of the parents joining hands with the schoolmaster appears very evidently, for when the master commands his pupils to employ their *leisure* time in getting some necessary parts of learning, their friends should not command them to forbear: And when they ought to be at school at the stated hours, they should not be sent an hour or two after, in the time of health, sometimes with a *lye* in their lips to excuse their *tardiness,* and sometimes with an order, and a brazen front to tell their master, *Their friends think it time enough to come to school at nine in the morning,* because the weather is a little cold, or because they must have their breakfast first. I say parents should not act so *indiscreetly,* because it clips the wings of the master's authority. It makes *boys* first despise and undervalue and then become unmannerly and impertinent to them; correction for which makes the tutor hated by the children, and then there naturally follows either a total disregard to business, or a general *carelessness* in every thing they do.

And while I am speaking of the Education of Children, I hope I shall be forgiven if I drop a word or two relating to the *fair sex:* It is a general remark that they are so unhappy as seldom to be found either to *spell, write* or *cypher* well. And the reason is very obvious, because they do not stay at their *writing schools* long enough. A year's education in *writing* is by many thought enough for *girls,* and by others it is thought time enough to put them to it when they are *eighteen* or *twenty* years of age; whereas by sad experience, both these are found to be, the one *too short,* and the other *too late.* The first is a time *too* short, because when they are taken from the *writing school* they generally forget what they learnt for want of *practice;* and the other *too late,* because then they are apt to look too forward, imagine all things will come of themselves without any trouble, and think they can learn a great deal in a little time; and when they find they cannot compass their ends so soon as they would, then every little *difficulty* discourages them. And hence it is that *adult persons* seldom improve in the first principles of *learning* so fast as younger ones. For a proof of this, I appeal to every *woman,* whether I am just in my *sentiments* or not. The woman who has had a *liberal education* this way, knows the advantages that arise from the ready *use* of the pen; and the woman who has learnt little or nothing of it, cannot but lament the *want* of it. *Girls* therefore ought to be put to the *writing school* as early *as boys,* and continued in it as long, and it may be reasonably be expected that both sexes should be alike ready at their *pen.* But for want of this, how often do we see *women,* when left to shift for themselves in the melancholy state of *widowhood* (and what woman knows that she shall not be left in the like situation?), obliged to leave their business to the management of others; sometimes to their great *loss,* and sometimes to their utter *ruin;* when, on the contrary, had they been ready at their *pen,* could *spell* well and understand *figures,* they might not only have saved themselves from *ruin,* but perhaps have been mistresses of *good fortunes.* Hence then may be drawn the following, but most *natural conclusion,* viz: ''The Education of Youth is of such vast importance, and of such singular use in the scene of life, that it visibly carries its recommendation along with it: For on it, in great measure, depends all that we hope to be: every perfection that a generous and well disposed mind would gladly arrive at: 'Tis this that stamps the distinction of mankind, and renders one man preferable to another: Is almost the very capacity of doing well; and remarkably adorns every point of life.'' (Watt's *Essay*) And as the great end of human learning is to teach a man to know himself, and thereby fit for the Kingdom of Heaven: So he that knows most, consequently is enabled to practice the best, and become an example to those, who know but little, or are quite ignorant of their duty.

I am,

Your and your Children's Well-wisher,

Thomas Dilworth

(from *The Schoolmaster's Assistant: Being a Compendium of Arithmetic,* Wilmington 1791. Courtesy of Historical Society of Delaware.)

Thomas Dilworth, Schoolmaster. (above)

Sample pages from Thomas Dilworth,
A New Guide to the English Tongue.
(following pages)

FAB. I. The BOY and his MOTHER.

A Little boy who went to School, ftole one of his School-fellow's horn-books, and brought it home to his mother ; who was fo far from correcting and difcouraging him upon account of the Theft, that fhe commended and gave him an apple for his pains. In procefs of time, as the child grew up to be a man, he accuftomed himfelf to greater robberies ; and at laft, being apprehended and committed to Goal, he was tried and condemned for felony. On the day of his execution as the officers were conducting him to the Gallows, he was attended by a vaft crowd of people, and among the reft by his mother, who came fighing, and fobbing along, and taking on extremely for her Son's unhappy fate ; which the criminal obferving, called to the Sheriff, and begged the favour of him, that he would give him leave to fpeak a word or two to his poor afflicted mother. The Sheriff, (as who would deny a dying man fo reafonable a requeft) gave him permiffion : and the felon, while as every one thought, he was whifpering fomething of importance to his mother, bit off her Ear, to the great offence and furprife of the whole affembly. What, fays they, was not this Villain contented with the impious facts which he has already committed, but that he muft increafe the number of them, by doing this violence to his mother ? Good people, replied he, I would not have ye be under a miftake ; that wicked woman deferves this, and even worfe at my Hands ; for if fhe had chaftifed and chid, inftead of rewarding and careffing me, when in my infancy I ftole the horn-book, from the School, I had not come to this ignominious untimely end.

The APPLICATION.

Though the depravity of man is very great, we do not fcruple to affirm that this depravity receives great addition from a bad education ; and that the child may charge either to the example or connivance of

FAB. III. The Fox and the GOAT.

A Fox having tumbled, by chance, into a well, had been casting about a long while, to no purpose, how he should get out again ; when, at last, a Goat came to the place, and wanting to drink, asked *Reynard,* whether the water was good ? Good ! says he, aye, so sweet, that I am afraid I have surfeited myself, I have drank so abundantly. The Goat, upon this, without any more ado, leapt in ; and the Fox, taking the advantage of his horns, by the assistance of them, as nimbly leapt out, leaving the poor Goat at the bottom of the well, to shift for himself.

The APPLICATION.

The doctrine taught us by this Fable is no more than this, That we ought to consider who it is that advises us, before we follow the advice. For, however plausible the counsel may seem, if the Person who gives it is a crafty knave, we may be assured that he intends to serve himself in it, more than us, if not to erect something to his own advantage out of our Ruin.

The poor little Country Attorney, ready to perish, and sunk into poverty, for the want of employment, draws a rich old farmer, a neighbour of his, into the gulph of the *Law* ; till laying hold of the branches of his revenue, he lifts himself out of obscurity, and leaves the other immured in the bottom of a Mortgage.

104 *A New Guide*

SENTENCES IN VERSE.

LIFE IS SHORT AND MISERABLE.
AH! few and full of sorrow are the days
Of miserable Man ; his life decays
Like that frail flower which with the sun's uprise,
Her bud unfolds, and with the evening dies ;
He like an empty shadow glides away,
And all his life is but a winter's day.

ON THE DILIGENT ANTS.
Ants in batalia to their cells convey,
The plundered forage of their yellow prey ;
The little drudges trot about and sweat,
But will not straight dovour all they get,
For in their mouths we see them carry home,
A stock for winter which they know must come.

ON THE ATHEIST.
Bold is the wretch, and blasphemous the man,
Who being finite, will attempt to scan
The works of him that's infinitely wise,
And those he cannot comprehend, denies.
Our reason is too weak a guide to show,
How God Almighty governs all below.

A FUTURE STATE CERTAIN
Brave youths the paths of virtue still should tread
And not by error's devious tract be led :
Till free from filth, and spotless is their mind,
Till pure their life, of th' ætherial kind :
For this we must believe when'er we die,
We sink to Hell, or else to Heaven fly.

HEAVENLY LOVE.
Christ's arms do still stand open to receive
All weary prodigals whom sin doth leave ;
For them he left his Father's blest abode,
Made son of man to make man son of God :
To cure their wounds he life's elixir-bled,
And dy'd a death to raise us from the dead.

THE SELF-WISE.
Conceited thoughts indulg'd without controul,
Exclude all further Knowledge from the Soul ;
For he who thinks himself already wise,
In course, all further knowledge will despise :
And but for this how many might have been
Just, reputable, wise, and honest men !

ON DEATH.
Death at a distance we but slightly fear,
He brings his terrors as he draws more near,
Through Poverty, Pain, Slav'ry we drudge on,
The worst of beings better please than none ?
No price too dear to purchase life and breath,
The heaviest burthen's easier borne than death.

Pages from a Popular Children's Book Reprinted in Wilmington in 1793.
(From the Charles Dorman Collection, Historical Society of Delaware.)

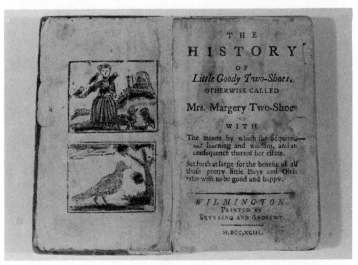

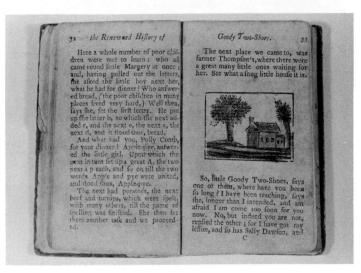

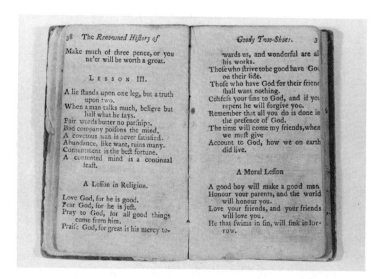

38   The *Renowned History of*

Make much of three pence, or you
    ne'er will be worth a groat.

LESSON III.

A lie stands upon one leg, but a truth
    upon two.
When a man talks much, believe but
    half what he says.
Fair words butter no parsnips.
Bad company poisons the mind.
A covetous man is never satisfied.
Abundance, like want, ruins many.
Contentment is the best fortune.
A contented mind is a continual
    feast.

A Lesson in Religion.

Love God, for he is good.
Fear God, for he is just.
Pray to God, for all good things
    come from him.
Praise God, for great is his mercy to-

Goody Two-Shoes.   3

wards us, and wonderful are all
    his works.
Those who strive to be good have God
    on their side.
Those who have God for their friend
    shall want nothing.
Confess your sins to God, and if you
    repent he will forgive you.
Remember that all you do is done in
    the presence of God.
The time will come my friends, when
    we must give
Account to God, how we on earth
    did live.

A Moral Lesson

A good boy will make a good man.
Honour your parents, and the world
    will honour you.
Love your friends, and your friends
    will love you.
He that swims in sin, will sink in sor-
    row.

SAMPLES OF HUMOR AND ANECDOTES FROM
THE FUNNY COMPANION
Printed in Wilmington in 1797

Dr. F—————, being in England in the year 1775
was asked by a nobleman, what would satisfy the Americans? He answered that it might easily be comprised in a few
re's, which he immediately wrote on a piece of paper. Thus:

-call your forces
-store Castle William
-pair the damage done to Boston
-peal your unconstitutional acts
-nounce your pretentions to taxes
-fund the duties you have extorted;
re   after this
-quire, and

-ceive payment for the destroyed tea,
   with the voluntary grants of the
   colonies, and then
-joice in a happy
-counciliation.

****

An old lady, who was not very much famed for good breeding and politeness, whatever other quality she might possess, being in a large party of very genteel company, happened to break wind backwards: a young gentleman who sat near her, seeing the company observe it, took the shame upon himself, and apologized very modestly for the rudeness he had been guilty of. It passed very well, and the next day the lady sent him a pair of colours, with her compliments, and this remark, "That it was an ill wind that blew nobody good."

****

A gentleman calling for small beer at another gentleman's table, finding it very hard, gave to the servant again without drinking. What, said the master of the house, do not you like the beer? It is not to be found fault with, answered the other, *for one should never speak ill of the dead.*

****

A jockey lately selling a nag to a gentleman, frequently observed with much earnestness, "that he was an *honest* horse." After the purchase, the gentleman asked him, "What he meant by an honest horse?" "Why I'll tell you," replied the jockey, "whenever I rode him he always threatened to throw me, and d—n if he ever *deceived* me."

****

A Methodist was giving a neighbour of his a lecture against swearing; assuring him that if he disregarded his admonition, and persisted in that wicked practice, he would certainly go to hell when he died. *If I do I'll be damn'd,* replied the other.

****

Some ladies walking in the meadows, a few miles from Wilmington, they met a shepherd with a young kid in his arms, one of whom stroaked and admired it, and asked the reason it had no horns. The shepherd, vexed at being detained, answered, "because he is not married."

Verses from *THE FUNNY COMPANION*

KITTY HARD TO PLEASE

I do not like a man that's tall;
A man that's little's worse than all.
I much abhor a man that's fat—
A man that's thin is worse than that.
A young man is a constant pest
An old one would my room infest.
I do not like a man that's fair,
A man that's black I cannot bear;
A man of sense I could not rule;
And from my heart I hate a fool;
A sober man I will not take—
A drunken man my heart would break;
All these I do sincerely hate,
And yet I love the married state.

ANSWER
BOB WHAT YOU PLEASE

Dear Kitty, I'm the man for thee,
    I'm neither tall nor slender,
Nor young nor old, come treat with me,
    I'm ready to surrender—

Nor grossly fat, nor ghostly spare,
    Not sedulous, nor slack miss—
Like puny boy I am not fair,
    Nor like an Indian black, miss—

Plain common sense I do not lack,
    And that's a lawful tender;
Yet I ne'er made an Almanack,
    Nor saw the witch of Endor.

No sober smock fac'd lump am I,
    That deems the bottle treason;
I'll stick to Bacchus 'till I die,
    But will not drown my reason.

A decent bowl inspires the soul,
    And makes us better spunk, miss;
But he's a brute beyond dispute,
    Who grogs it till he's drunk, miss;

So Kitty if I please your mind,
    With you I'd like to winter—
And when you wish my place to find,
    Enquire of the Printer.

(From *The Funny Companion*, 134, 135. Courtesy of the
Wilmington Library.)

AN ACT TO INCORPORATE THE MEMBERS
OF THE LIBRARY COMPANY OF WILMINGTON*
[PREAMBLE]

Whereas John Dickinson, Thomas May, Charles H. Wharton, Jacob Broom, Joseph Warner, John Ferris, John Hayes, William Poole, James Robinson, jun., Isaac Hendrickson, Isaac Starr, jun., John Springer, Eli Mendinhall, James Lea, jun., John Thelwell, James Brobson, Henry Paschall, Israel Brown, Samuel Brynes, Thomas Robinson, William Robinson, Patrick Murdoch, John Martin, Frederick Craig, John Shallcross, Nicholas Way, Peter Brynberg, John Moore, George Clark, Francis Way, Henry Reynolds, Ebenezer A. Smith, Joshua Jackson, Sarah Frisby, Philip Bonsall, William Sharply, jun., William Corbitt, Daniel J. Adams, Joseph Capelle, John M'Kinly, Gunning Bedford, jun., John Rumsey, Joseph Summerl, Joseph Shipley, James Delaplain, Jehu Hollingworth, jun., Thomas Lea and Isaac Starr have by their petition to this general assembly set forth, ''That they have at a considerable expence, purchased a large and valuable collection of useful books, in order to erect a Library in the borough of Wilmington, for the advancement of knowledge and literature, and have formed themselves into a company by the name of THE LIBRARY COMPANY OF WILMINGTON; and prayed that the said company may be incorporated, and by law enabled, as a body politic and corporate, to receive and hold such donations and bequests as may from time to time be made to the said company, and vested with such powers and privileges as the nature of the institution shall require: And this general assembly being truly sensible of the advantage that may accrue to the people of this state, by so laudable and useful an undertaking, and being willing to encourage the same:

Be it therefore enacted, by the general assembly of Delaware, [That the said persons named above] and such other persons as shall hereafter be admitted, or become members of the

Library Company of Wilmington, according to the laws and constitutions of the said company, hereafter to be made, be, and forever hereafter shall be, by virtue of these presents, one body, politic and corporate in deed, fact, name, and in law, to have the continuance forever by the name, stile and title of THE LIBRARY COMPANY OF WILMINGTON.

A Catalogue of Books Belonging
To the Library Company of Wilmington, ca. 1800

NUMBER	TITLE	VOLS.
	Atlas	1
100	Annual Register	23
71	Accomplished Woman	2
73	American Museum	5
12	Animated Nature	8
61	Age of Lewis XV	2
	Aphorisms on Man	1
136	Anderson on National Industry	2
1	American Magazine	6
135	Anderson's British Embassy	1
	Abolition Society	1
52	Antipedo Rantims	1
109	Appeal to Scripture, Reason and Tradition	1
29	Adam's Modern Travels	2
167	Anacharsis's Travels	5
265	Annual Register	18
265	Annual Register for 1798	1
271	Anderson Agriculture	1
273	Ancient Europe	2
286	Abstract Account of Louisiana	1
296	Art and Nature	1
312	Austin's Letters	1
	Anderson's Recreations in Agriculture	1
	Architecture by Biddle	1
	American Citizen	1

103	Bruce's Travels	6
	Ditto abridged	
17	Bell's Travels in Tartary	2
119	Blackstone's Commentaries	5
195	Bates on Man's Redemption	1
7	Brydone's Tour	2
224	Bancroft's Guianna	1
10	Buffon's Natural History	9
66	Benezet's Account of Guinea	1
2	Bourgoanne's Spain	3
104	Boston Academy	1
109	Bartram's Travels	1
115	Burlamaque	1
111	Bank's Geography and Maps	3
18	Bennet's Letters	1
134	Belsham's George the Illid	4
221	Benyouskey's Travels	2
241	Biographical Dictionary	8
177	Brackenridge's Incidents of the	1
	Western Insurrection	
165	Belsham's Essays	4
262	Belknap's American Biography	2
300	Blair's Sermons	2
	Burn's Works	3
	Beddoes Observations	1
	Brown's Travels	1
	Blair's Lectures	2
126	Cook's Voyages	3
208	Carver's Travels	1
91	Cox's Travels	3
69	Chapone's Letters	1
96	Caspipina's Letters	1
9	Chenier's History of Morocco	2
84	Christie's Letters	1
35	Craftsman	7

3	Cox's Switzerland	2
	Clarkson's Essays on Slave Trade	1
80	Cox's View of the U. States	1
	of America	
214	Cicero's Orations	1
	Connecticut Claims	1
227	Corruption of the Fathers	1
22	Caleb Williams	2
163	Cheap Repository	1
169	Chaptall's Chemistry	1
260	Count Rumford's Essays	2
189	Cornaro on Health	1
272	Catharine 2d of Russia	2
284	Campbell's Narrative	
294	Causticks' Tractoration	2
305	Cowper's Poems	2
	Carr's Northern Summer	1
	Stranger in France	1
	ditto in Ireland	1
	Collection of Disastrous Voyages	1
	Citizen of the World	2
76	Dillon's Travels	1
120	Dictionaire by Bayle	4
48	D'Argenson's Works	1
232	Delome on the British Constitution	1
160	Derham's Works	1
121	DuHald's History of China	1
92	Dow's History of Hindostan	3
63	De Tott's Memoirs	3
213	Dissertation on Pure Love	1
216	Dumourier's Memoirs	1
211	Demosthenes's Orations	3
238	Dissertations on Asia	1
255	Darwin's Zoonomia	2
269	Do. Phytologia	1
268	Do. Botanick Garden	1

8	Gentleman's Magazine	2
26	Gustavus Vassa	1
74	Guardian	2
141	Gillie's History of Greece	3
112	Guthrie's Geography	2
	Maps	2
251	Gregory's Essays	1
186	Gallery of Portraits	1
	Goldsmith's Poems	1
	Goldsmith's Essays	2
138	Hume's History of England with Smollet's continuation	14
122	Howard on Prisons	1
82	History of California	2
23	Harvey's Dialogues	3
102	History of Mexico	3
87	Historical Review of Pennsylvania	1
77	Hanway's Travels	2
83	Handmaid to the Arts	2
89	Humphrey's Works	1
95	Hopkinson's Works	3
116	Herrington's Works	1
65	History of Florence	1
44	History of Jamaica	1
205	History of Poland	1
240	Hooper's Recreations	4
31	Homer's Illiad and Odissey	2
27	Hool's Tasso	2
235	History of China	2
261	History of Pennsylvania	2
	Maps to ditto	1
266	History of France	4
275	Hawkin's Appeal	1
290	Hope and memory	1
	Hamilton on Education	2

289   Link's Travels   1
302   Life of Christ   2
304   Life of Lady Guion   1
311   Letters from Europe by a Pennsylvanian   2
301   Life of Washington   5
      Life of Johnson   1
      Life of Jardnier   1
      Literary Magazine   4

56   Moore's Travels   5
194   Memorial of Facts   1
70   Mighty Destroyer   1
42   Marshall's Travels   1
159   Moore's Utopia   1
57   Montesquieu's Spirit of Laws   2
79   Morse's Geography   1
43   Messiah by Klobstock   1
75   Mirabeau's Letters de Cachet   1
94   Minute Philosopher   2
196   Monroe's View   1
239   Milwright and Millers Guide   1
32   Moore's Journal
15   Mirror   2
38   Mahomet's Travels   2
203   Modern Europe   5
30   Maria William's Letters, 5 vols. in   3
236   St. Mery's St. Domingo   2
170   Murphy's Tacitus   4
256   Monthly Magazine   2
256   Monthly Magazine for 1799   2
256   Monthly Magazine for 1800   1
267   Monthly Magazine and American Review   3
280   Mackinzie's Travels   1
290   Millar's Retrospect   6
293   Monthly Visitor   17
295   Monsceau's Practical Husbandry   1
299   Meditations, Sacramental   1

307	New Monthly Magazine	10
315	M'Hahor's Gardner	1
301	Mackinzie's Second Tour	1
	Majiors Visages	22
171	Newton on Prophecy, 1st & 3d	2
28	Necker on Religious Opinions	1
148	Nicolson's Philosophy	1
314	Nicolson's Journal	1
139	Origin of Laws	3
	Observation on Novel Reading	1
199	Political Justice	2
218	Park on Insurance	1
200	Priestley's Lectures	1
246	Poffendorf's History of Europe	2
85	Price on Annuities	1
54	Pope's Works	6
49	Paradise Lost	1
47	Pelew Islands (account of)	1
37	Pindar Peter	2
193	Paley's Philosophy	1
233	Page's Travels	1
5	Phillip's Voyage	1
4	Piozzi's Travels	1
229	Practical Farmer	1
245	Paine's Works	1
154	Pennington on Chymistry	1
176	Paley's Evidences	1
181	Plutarch's Lives	6
191	Primitive Physick	1
370	Parke's Travels	1
285	Paley's Theology	1
313	Plowden's History of Ireland	5
	Pleasure of Imagination	1
105	Robertson's Charles the Vth	3

36	Thompson's Seasons	1
25	Tully's Offices	1
156	Tissot on Health	1
24	Travels in Europe, Asia and Africa	2
59	Travels of a Philosopher	1
106	Transactions of the American Philosophical Society	1
58	Tattler	4
180	Trials of Rowen, Gerald and Muir	1
	Task, a poem	1
118	Universal Traveller	1
125	Universal Magazine	8
222	Ulloa's Voyages	2
20	Voltair's Universal History	1
207	Vaillant's Travels	1
68	Valuable Secrets	1
86	Varieties of Literature	2
197	Vattal's Law of Nations	1
283	Van Braam's Embassy to China	2
234	Wraxall's Tour	1
77	Ward's Dissertations	1
147	Warson's History of the Philips, IId and IIId, Kings of Spain	3
146	War in America	
174	Weekly Magazine	1
198	Washington's Letters	2
33	Warville on Commerce	1
161	Watt's Logic	1
88	Wyndham's Travels	4
98	Watson's Apology	1
155	Wendeborn's England	2
253	Wilberforce's View	1
259	Winterbottom's America	4
259	And Maps	1

*At first glance the date of this catalogue of books would appear to be 1788, the year when the library was incorporated, but internal evidence indicates otherwise. Hugh Brackenridge's volume on the western insurrections was first printed in 1795, and Dr. Benjamin Rush issued his book on yellow fever in 1793. Printed items with dates include the "Monthly Magazine for 1799" and "Monthly Magazine for 1800." Nevertheless it is a valuable list of popular books being read by Delawareans by the end of the eighteenth century, even though Shakespeare is missing!

(Courtesy of the Wilmington Library, Wilmington, Delaware)

THE CONSTITUTION
OF DELAWARE, 1776

THE CONSTITUTION OR SYSTEM OF GOVERNMENT, AGREED TO AND RESOLVED UPON BY THE REPRE-SENTATIVES IN FULL CONVENTION OF THE DELA-WARE STATE, FORMERLY STILED THE GOVERNMENT OF THE COUNTIES OF NEW-CASTLE, KENT AND SUS-SEX, UPON DELAWARE, THE SAID REPRESENTATIVES BEING CHOSEN BY THE FREEMEN OF THE SAID STATE FOR THAT EXPRESS PURPOSE.

Article 1. The government of the Counties of New-Castle, Kent and Sussex, upon Delaware, shall hereafter in all Public And other Writings be called, THE DELAWARE STATE.

2. THE Legislature shall be formed of two distinct Branches:— They shall meet once or oftener in every Year, and shall be called, THE GENERAL ASSEMBLY OF DELAWARE.

3. One of the Branches of the Legislature shall be called, THE HOUSE OF ASSEMBLY, and shall consist of seven Representatives, to be chosen for each County annually of such Persons as are Freeholders of the same.

4. The other Branch shall be called, THE COUNCIL, and consist of nine Members, three to be chosen for each County at the Time of the first Election of the Assembly, who shall be Freeholders of the County for which they are chosen, and be upwards of twenty-five Years of Age. At the End of one Year after the General Election, the Counsellor who had the small-est Number of Votes in each County shall be displaced, and the Vacancies thereby occasioned supplied by the Freemen of each County choosing the same or another Person at a new Election in Manner aforesaid. At the End of two Years after the first General Election, the Counsellor who stood second in Number of Votes in each County shall be displaced and the Vacancies thereby occasioned supplied by a new Election in Manner aforesaid. And at the End of three Years from the first general Election, the Counsellor who had the greatest

Number of Votes in each County shall be displaced, and the Vacancies thereby occasioned supplied by a new Election in Manner aforesaid. And this Rotation of a Counsellor being displaced at the End of three Years in each County and his Office supplied by a new Choice shall be continued afterwards in due Order annually forever, whereby, after the first general Election a Counsellor will remain in Trust for three Years from the Time of his being elected, and a Counsellor will be displaced, and the same or another chosen in each County at every Election.

5. THE Right of Suffrage in the Election of Members for both Houses shall remain as exercised by Law at present; and each House shall choose its own Speaker, appoint its own Officers, judge of the Qualifications and Elections of its own Members, settle its own Rules of Proceedings and direct Writs of Election for supplying intermediate Vacancies. They may also severally expel any of their own Members for Misbehaviour, but not a second Time in the same Sessions for the same Offence, if re-elected; and they shall have all other Powers necessary for the Legislature of a free and Independent State.

6. ALL Money-Bills for the Support of Government shall originate in the House of Assembly, and may be altered, amended or rejected by the Legislative Council. All other Bills and Ordinances may take Rise in the House of Assembly or Legislative Council, and may be altered, amended or rejected by either.

7. A PRESIDENT, or Chief Magistrate shall be chosen by joint Ballot of both Houses, to be taken in the House of Assembly, and the Box examined by the Speaker of each House in the Presence of the other Members, and in Case the Numbers for the two highest in Votes should be equal, then the Speaker of the Council shall have an additional casting Voice, and the Appointment of the Person who has the Major-

ity of Votes shall be entered at large on the Minutes and Journals of each House, and a Copy thereof on Parchment, certified and signed by the Speaker respectively, and sealed with the Great-Seal of the State, which they are hereby authorized to affix, shall be delivered to the Person so chosen President, who shall continue in that Office three Years and until the Sitting of the next General Assembly and no longer, nor be eligible until the Expiration of three Years after he shall have been out of that Office. An adequate but moderate Salary shall be settled on him during his continuance in Office.—He may draw for such Sums of Money as shall be appropriated by the General Assembly, and be accountable to them for the same.—He may by and with the Advice of the Privy-Council lay Embargoes or prohibit the Exportation of any Commodity for any Time not exceeding thirty Days in the Recess of the General Assembly.—He shall have the Power of granting Pardons or Reprieves, except where the Prosecution shall be carried on by the House of Assembly, or the Law shall otherwise direct, in which Cases no Pardon or Reprieve shall be granted but by a Resolve of the House of Assembly:—And may exercise all the other executive Powers of Government, limited and restrained as by this Constitution is mentioned, and according to the Laws of the State. And on his Death, inability or Absence from the State, the Speaker* of the House of Assembly shall have the Powers of a President until a new Nomination is made by the General Assembly.

8. A PRIVY-COUNCIL consisting of four Members shall be chosen by Ballot, two by the Legislative Council, and two by the House of Assembly: Provided, that no regular Officer of the Army or Navy in the Service and Pay of the Continent, or of this, or any other State shall be eligible. And a Member of the Legislative Council or of the House of Assembly being

---

*Of the Legislative Council for the Time being shall be Vice-President, and in case of his Death, Inability or absence from the State.

chosen of the Privy-Council and accepting thereof shall thereby lose his Seat. Three Members shall be a Quorum, and their Advice and Proceedings shall be entered of Record and signed by the Members present, (to any Part of which any Member may enter his Dissent) to be laid before the General Assembly when called for by them. Two Members shall be removed by Ballot, one by the Legislative Council and one by the House of Assembly at the End of Two Years, and those who remain the next Year after, who shall severally be ineligible for the three next Years. These Vacancies as well as those occasioned by Death or Incapacity shall be supplied by new Elections in the same Manner. And this Rotation of a Privy-Counsellor shall be continued afterwards in due Order annually forever. The President may by Summons convene the Privy-Council at any Time when the Public Exigences may require, and at such Place as he shall think most convenient, when and where they are to attend accordingly.

9. THE president, with the Advice and Consent of the Privy-Council, may embody the Militia, and act as Captain-General and Commander in Chief of them and the other Military Force of this State under the Laws of the same.

10. EITHER House of the General Assembly may adjourn themselves respectively. The President shall not prorogue, adjourn or dissolve the General Assembly, but he may with the Advice of the Privy-Council or on the Application of a Majority of either House, call them before the Time they shall stand Adjourned, and the two Houses shall always sit at the same Time and Place, for which Purpose immediately after every adjournment the Speaker of the House of Assembly shall give Notice to the Speaker of the House of the Time to which the House of Assembly stands adjourned.

11. THE DELEGATES FOR DELAWARE to the Congress of the UNITED STATES OF AMERICA shall be chosen annually, or superseded in the mean Time, by joint Ballot of both Houses in the General Assembly.

12. THE President and General Assembly shall by joint Ballot appoint three Justices of the Supreme Court for the State, one of whom shall be Chief-Justice, and a Judge of Admiralty, and also four Justices of the Courts of Common Pleas and Orphans Courts for each County, one of whom in each Court shall be stiled Chief Justice, (and in Case of Division on the Ballot, the President shall have an additional casting Voice) to be commissioned by the President under the Great-Seal, who shall continue in Office during good Behaviour; and during the Time the Justices of the said Supreme Court and Courts of Common Pleas remain in Office they shall hold none other except in the Militia—Any one of the Justices of either of said Courts shall have power in Case of the non-coming of his brethren to open and adjourn the Court. An adequate fixed but moderate salary shall be settled on them during their Continuance in Office. The President and Privy-Council shall appoint the Secretary, the Attorney-General, Registers for the Probate of Wills and granting Letters of Administration, Registers in Chancery, Clerks of the Courts of Common-Pleas and Orphans Courts, and Clerks of the Peace, who shall be commissioned as aforesaid and remain in Office during five Years, if they behave themselves well; during which Time the said Registers in Chancery and Clerks shall not be Justices of either of the said Courts of which they are Officers, but they shall have Authority to sign all Writs by them issued, and take Recoginances of Bail. The Justices of the Peace shall be nominated by the House of Assembly, that is to say, They shall name twenty-four Persons for each County, of whom the President, with the Approbation of the Privy-Council, shall appoint twelve, who shall be commissioned as aforesaid, and continue in Office during seven Years, if they behave themselves well; and in Case of Vacancies, or if the Legislature shall think proper to increase the Number, they shall be nominated and appointed in like Manner. The Members of the Legislative and Privy-Councils shall be Justices of the Peace for the whole State, during their Continuance in Trust; and the Justices of the Courts of Com-

mon Pleas shall be conservators of the Peace in their respective Counties.

13. THE Justices of the Courts of Common-Pleas and Orphans Courts shall have the Power of holding Inferior Courts of Chancery as heretofore, unless the Legislature shall otherwise direct.

14. THE Clerks of the Supreme Court shall be appointed by the Chief Justice thereof, and the Recorders of Deeds by the Justices of The Courts of Common-Pleas for each County severally, and commissioned by the President under the Great-Seal, and continue in Office five Years, if they behave themselves well.

15. THE Sheriffs and Coroners of the respective Counties shall be chosen annually as heretofore; and any Person having served three Years as Sheriff shall be ineligible for three Years after; and the President and Privy-Council shall have the Appointment of such of the two Candidates returned for said Offices of Sheriff and Coroner as they shall think best qualified, in the same Manner that the Governor heretofore enjoyed this Power.

16. THE General Assembly by joint Ballot shall appoint the Generals and Field-Officers, and all the other Officers in the Army or Navy of this State. And the President may appoint during Pleasure, until otherwise directed by the Legislature, all necessary Civil Officers not herein before mentioned.

17. THERE shall be an Appeal from the Supreme Court of Delaware in Matters of Law and Equity to a Court of seven Persons, to consist of the President for the Time being, who shall preside therein, and six others, to be appointed, three by the Legislative Council and three by the House of Assembly, who shall continue in Office during good Behaviour, and be commissioned by the President under the Great-Seal; which

Court shall be stiled, The Court of Appeals, and have all the Authority and Powers theretofore given by Law in the last Resort to the King in Council under the old Government. The Secretary shall be the Clerk of this Court, and Vacancies therein occasioned by Death or Incapacity shall be supplied by new Elections in Manner aforesaid.

18. THE Justices of the Supreme Court and Courts of Common-Pleas, the Members of the Privy-Council, the Secretary, the Trustees of the Loan-Office and Clerks of the Courts of Common-Pleas, during their continuance in Office, and all Persons concerned in any Army or Navy Contracts, shall be ineligible to either House of Assembly; and any Member of either House accepting of any other of the Offices herein before mentioned (excepting the Office of a Justice of the Peace) shall have his Seat thereby vacated, and a new Election shall be ordered.

19. THE Legislative Council and Assembly shall have the Power of making the Great-Seal of this State, which shall be kept by the President, or in his Absence by the Vice-President, to be used by them as Occasion may require. It shall be called, The Great-Seal of the Delaware State, and shall be affixed to all Laws and Commissions.

20. COMMISSIONS shall run in the Name of THE DELAWARE STATE, and bear Test by the President, Writs shall run in the same Manner, and bear Test in the Name of the Chief-Justice or Justice first named in the Commissions for the several Courts, and be sealed with the Public Seals of such Courts. Indictments shall conclude, against the peace and Dignity of the State.

21. IN Case of Vacancy of the Offices above directed to be filled by the President and General Assembly, the President and Privy-Council may appoint others in their Stead until there shall be a new Election.

22. EVERY Person, who shall be chosen a Member of either House, or appointed to any Office or Place of Trust, before taking his Seat, or entering upon the Execution of his Office, shall take the following Oath, or Affirmation if conscientiously scrupulous of taking an Oath, to wit.

"I A. B. will bear true Allegiance to the Delaware State, sub-
"mit to its Constitution and Laws, and do no Act wittingly
"whereby the Freedom thereof may be prejudiced."

And also make and subscribe the following Declaration, to wit.
"I A. B. do profess Faith in God the Father, and in Jesus Christ
"his only Son, and in the Holy Ghost, one God blessed for ever-
"more; and I do acknowledge the Holy Scriptures of the Old
"and New Testament to be given by divine Inspiration."

And all Officers shall also take an Oath of Office.

23. THE President when he is out of Office and within eighteen Months after, and all others, offending against the State either by Mal-Administration, Corruption or other Means, by which the Safety of the Commonwealth may be endangered, within eighteen Months after the Offence committed, shall be impeachable by the House of Assembly before the Legislative Council; Such Impeachment to be prosecuted by the Attorney-General or such other Persons or Persons as the House of Assembly may appoint, according to the Laws of the Land. If found Guilty, he or they shall be forever disabled to hold any Office under Government, or removed from Office pro-tempore, or subjected to such Pains and Penalties as the Laws shall direct. And all Officers shall be removed on Conviction of Misbehaviour at Common Law or on Impeachment, or upon the Address of the General Assembly.

24. ALL Acts of Assembly in Force in this State on the fifteenth Day of May last (and not hereby altered, or contrary to the Resolutions of Congress, or of the late House of

Assembly of this State) shall so continue until altered or repealed by the Legislature of this State, unless where they are temporary, in which Case they shall expire at the Time respectively limited for their Duration.

25. THE Common Law of England, as well as so much of the Statute Law as have been heretofore adopted in Practice in this State, shall remain in force, unless they shall be altered by future Law of the Legislature; such Parts only excepted as are repugnant to the Rights and Privileges contained in this Constitution and the Declaration of Rights, &c. agreed to by this Convention.

26. No Person hereafter imported into this State from Africa ought to be held in Slavery under any Pretence whatever, and no Negro, Indian or Mulatto Slave, ought to be brought into this State for Sale from any part of the World.

27. THE first Election for the General Assembly of this State shall be held on the twenty-first Day of October next, at the Court Houses in the several Counties, in the Manner heretofore used in the Election of the Assembly, except as to the Choice of Inspectors and Assessors, where Assessors have not been chosen on the sixteenth Day of September instant, which shall be made on the Morning of the Day of Election by the Electors, Inhabitants of the respective Hundreds in each County;—At which Time the Sheriffs and Coroners for the said Counties respectively are to be elected: And the present Sheriffs of the Counties of New-Castle and Kent may be re-chosen to that Office until the first Day of October in the Year of our Lord One Thousand Seven Hundred and Seventy-nine, and the present Sheriff for the County of Sussex may be re-chosen to that Office until the first Day of October in the Year of our Lord One Thousand Seven Hundred and Seventy-eight, provided the Freemen think proper to re-elect them at every general Election; and the present Sheriffs and Coroners respectively shall continue to exercise

their Offices as heretofore until the Sheriffs and Coroners to be elected on the said twenty-first Day of October shall be commissioned and sworn into Office. The Members of the Legislative Council and Assembly shall meet for transacting the business of the State on the twenty-eighth Day of October next, and continue in Office until the first Day of October which will be in the Year One Thousand Seven Hundred and Seventy-seven; on which Day, and on the first Day of October in each Year forever after, the Legislative Council, Assembly, Sheriffs and Coroners, shall be chosen by Ballot in Manner directed by the several Laws of this State for regulating Elections of Members of Assembly and Sheriffs and Coroners; and the General Assembly shall meet on the twentieth Day of the same Month for transacting the Business of the State; and if any of the said first and twentieth Days of October should be Sunday, then and in such Case the Elections shall be held and the General Assembly meet the next Day following.

28. To prevent any Violence or Force being used at the said Elections, no Persons shall come armed to any of them; and no Muster of the Militia shall be made on that Day, nor shall any Battalion or Company give in their Votes immediately succeeding each other, if any other Voter who offers to vote objects thereto, nor shall any Battalion or Company in the Pay of the Continent, or of this or any other State, be suffered to remain at the Time and Place of holding the said Elections, nor within one Mile of the said Places respectively for twenty-four Hours before the opening said Elections, nor within twenty-four Hours after the same are closed, so as in any Manner to impede the freely and conveniently carrying on the said Election: Provided always, that every Elector may in a peaceable and orderly Manner give in his Vote on the said Day of Election.

29. THERE shall be no Establishment of any one Religious Sect in this State in Preference to another; and no Clergyman

or Preacher of the Gospel of any Denomination shall be capable of holding any Civil Office in this State, or of being a Member of either of the Branches of the Legislature while they continue in the Exercise of the Pastoral function.

30. No Article of the Declaration of Rights and Fundamental Rules of this State, agreed to by this Convention, nor the first, second, fifth (except that Part thereof that relates to the Right of Suffrage) twenty-sixth and twenty-ninth Articles of this Constitution, ought ever to be violated on any Prentence whatever. No other Part of this Constitution shall be altered, changed or diminished, without the Consent of five Parts in Seven of the Assembly, and seven Members of the Legislative Council.

(This item and the Bill of Rights below, *Proceedings of the Convention of the Delaware State on Tuesday the 27th of August, 1776*. Reprint Star Publishing Co., Wilmington, Delaware, 1927.)

THE BILL OF RIGHTS

A DECLARATION OF RIGHTS AND FUNDAMENTAL RULES OF THE DELAWARE STATE, FORMERLY STILED THE GOVERNMENT OF THE COUNTIES OF NEW-CASTLE, KENT AND SUSSEX, UPON DELAWARE

1. That all Government of Right originates from the People, is founded in Compact only, and instituted solely for the Good of the Whole.
2. That all Men have a natural and unalienable Right to worship Almighty God according to the Dictates of their Consciences and Understandings; and that no Man ought, or of Right can be compelled, to attend any religious Worship or maintain any Ministry to or against his own free Will and Consent, and that no Authority can or ought to be vested in, or assumed by any Power whatever, that shall in any case interfere with or in any Manner controul

the Right of Conscience in the free Exercise of religious Worship.

3. That all Persons professing the Christian Religion ought forever to enjoy equal Rights and Privileges in this State, unless under Colour of Religion any Man disturb the Peace, the Happiness or Safety of Society.

4. That the People of this State have the sole, exclusive and Inherent Right of governing and regulating the internal Police of the same.

5. That Persons intrusted with the Legislative and Executive Powers are the Trustees and Servants of the Public, and as such accountable for their Conduct; wherefore whenever the Ends of Government are perverted, and Public Liberty manifestly endangered by the Legislative singly, or a treacherous Combination of both, the People may and of Right ought to, establish a new or reform the old Govenment.

6. That the Right in the People to participate in the Legislature is the Foundation of Liberty and of all free Government, and for this End all Elections ought to be free and frequent, and every Freeman having sufficient Evidence of a permanent common Interest with, and Attachment to, the Community, hath a Right of Suffrage.

7. That no Power of suspending Laws, or the Execution of Laws, ought to be exercised, unless by the Legislature.

8. That for Redress of Grievances and for amending and strengthening of the Laws, the Legislature ought to be frequently convened.

9. That every Man hath a Right to petition the Legislature for the Redress of Grievances in a peaceable and orderly manner.

10. That every member of Society hath a Right to be protected in the Enjoyment of Life, Liberty and Property, and therefore is bound to contribute his Proportion towards the Expence of that Protection, and yield his personal Service when necessary, or an Equivalent thereto; but no Part of a Man's Property can be justly taken from

him, or applied to public Uses, without his own Consent
or that of his Legal Represensatives: Nor can any Man
that is unconscientiously scrupulous of bearing Arms in
any Case be justly compelled thereto if he will pay such
Equivalent.

11. That retrospective Laws, punishing Offences committed
before the Existence of such Laws, are oppressive and
unjust, and ought not to be made.

12. That every Freeman for every Injury done him in his
Goods, Lands or Person, by any other Person, ought to
have Remedy by the Course of the Law of the Land, and
ought to have Justice and Right for the Injury done to
him freely without Sale, fully without any Denial, and
speedily without Delay, according to the Law of the
Land.

13. That Trial by Jury of Facts where they arise is one of the
greatest Securities of the Lives, Liberties and Estates of
the People.

14. That in all Prosecutions for criminal Offences, every
Man hath a Right to be informed of the Accusation
against him, to be allowed Counsel, to be confronted
with the Accusers or Witnesses, to examine Evidence on
Oath in his Favour and to a speedy Trial by an impartial
Jury, without whose unanimous Consent he ought not to
be found Guilty.

15. That no Man in the Courts of common Law ought to be
compelled to give evidence against himself.

16. That excessive Bail ought not to be required, nor excessive Fines imposed, nor cruel or unusual Punishments
inflicted.

17. That all Warrants without Oath to search suspected Places
or to seize any Person or his Property, are grievous and
oppressive, and all general Warrants to search suspected
Places, or to apprehend all Persons suspected without
naming or describing the Place or any Person in special,
are illegal and ought not to be granted.

18. That a well regulated Militia is the property, natural and safe Defence of a free Government.
19. That standing Armies are dangerous to Liberty, and ought not to be raised or kept up without the Consent of the Legislature.
20. That in all Cases and at all Times the Military ought to be under strict Subordination to and governed by the Civil Power.
21. That no Soldier ought to be quartered in any House in Time of Peace without the Consent of the Owner; and in Time of War in such manner only as the Legislature shall direct.
22. That the Independency and Uprightness of Judges are essential to the impartial Administration of Justice, and a great Security to the Rights and Liberties of the People.
23. That the Liberty of the Press ought to be inviolably preserved.

THE RAISING
A SONG FOR FEDERAL MECHANICS
by Francis Hopkinson, Esq.

Come muster, my lads, your mechanical tools,
Your saws and your axes, your hammer and rules:
Bring your mallets and plane, your level and line,
And plenty of pins of American [pine]
For our roof we will raise, and our song still shall be—
A government firm, and our citizens free.

Come, up with the plates, lay them firm on the wall,
Like one people at large, they're the ground-work for all;
Examine them well, and see that they're sound;
Let no rotten part in our building be found;
For our roof we will raise, and our song still shall be—
Our government firm, and our citizens free.

Now hand up the girders, lay each in its place,
Between them the joints must divide all the space;
Like assemblymen, these should lie level along,
Like girders, our senate prove loyal and strong.
For our roof we will raise, and our song still shall be—
A government firm, our citizens free.

The rafters now frame—your king-posts and braces,
And drive your pins home, to keep all in their places;
        Let wisdom and strength in the fabric combine,
And your pins be all made of American pine;
For our roof we will raise, and our song still shall be—
A government firm, our citizens free.

Our king-posts are judges—how upright they stand,
Supporting the braces, the laws of the land!
The laws of the land, which divide right from wrong,
And strengthen the weak, by weak'ning the strong;
For our roof we will raise, and our song still shall be—
Laws equal and just, for a people that's free.

Up! up with the rafters—each frame is a state!
How nobly they rise! their span, too, how great!
From the north to the south, o'er the whole they extend,
And rest on the walls, while the walls they defend!
For our roof we will raise, and our song still shall be—
Combined in strength, yet as citizens free.

Now enter the purlins, and drive your pins through,
And see that our joints are drawn home, and all true;
The purlins will bind all the rafters together,
The strength of the whole shall defy wind and weather:
For our roof we will raise, and our song still shall be—
United as states, but as citizens free.

Come raise up the turret—our glory and pride—
In the center it stands, o'er the whole to preside;

The sons of Columbia shall view with delight,
Its pillars, and arches, and towering height:
Our roof is now raised, and our song still shall be—
A federal head, o'er a people still free.

Huzza! my brave boys, our work is complete,
The world shall admire Columbia's fair seat;
Its strength against tempests and time shall be proof,
And thousands shall come to dwell under our Roof.
While we drain the deep bowl, our toast still shall be—
Our government firm, and our citizens free.

Thomas Fox, *The Wilmington Almanack, or Ephemeris, for the Year of our Lord, 1790,* Wilmington [1789]. Courtesy of Historical Society of Delaware.

BIBLIOGRAPHY

Of necessity, the following lists of books, articles and manuscripts is limited and by no means includes all the items consulted. The staff members at the Delaware State Archives, Historical Society of Delaware, Hagley Library, Special Collections at the University of Delaware, and Wilmington Public Library were helpful, gracious, and hospitable, as always.

In the Delaware State Archives the Probate Records, including inventories, assessment lists, the Ridgely family collection, the autobiography of William Morgan, and items in the General Reference Collection were of assistance. In the Historical Society of Delaware, the Rodney Collection, Morse Collection, newspapers of the 1780s and 1790s, both original and on microfilm, Wilmington imprints, and genealogical materials were consulted. In the Wilmington Public Library and in Special Collections of the Morris Library of the Unviversity of Delaware, I used Wilmington imprints. At the Hagley Library I consulted Wilmington imprints and maps.

Students of Delaware history are indebted to H. Clay and Marion Bjornson Reed for preparing *A Bibliography of Delaware History through 1960* (1966) and to members of the Reference department of the Morris Library for continuing it through 1974. Indispensable is Evald Rink, *Printing in Delaware, 1761–1800* (1969).

General histories include J. Thomas Scharf, *History of Delaware* (2 v.; 1888); Henry C. Conrad, *History of the State of Delaware* (3 v.; 1907); H. Clay Reed and Marion Bjornson Reed, eds., *Delaware: A History of the First State (3 v.; 1947);* Carol E Hoffecker, *Delaware: A Bicentennial History* (1977); John A. Munroe, *History of Delaware* (1979); and William H. Williams, *The First State: An Illustrated History* (1985). Dr. Munroe has also written *Colonial Delaware: A History* (1979).

In his research and writing Dr. Munroe has covered this period thoroughly. By far the most valuable published volume on the period in his *Federalist Delaware, 1775-1815* (1954), which deals with all aspects of life in the 1780s. Munroe also wrote the section on the Revolution and the subsequent period in Reed's *History, supra,* 1: 95-124; "Reflections on Delaware and the American Revolution," *Delaware History,* 17: 1-11 (1976); and "The Philadelawareans: A Study of Relations between Philadelphia and Delaware in the Late Eighteenth Century," *Pennsylvania Magazine of History and Biography,* 69: 128-149 (1945). In addition, he has also edited *Timoleon's Biographical History of Dionysius: Tyrant of Delaware* (1958) and edited with R.O. Bausman, "James Tilton's Notes on the Agriculture of Delaware in 1788," *Agricultural History,* 20: 176-187 (1946).

Studies of this period by Dr. Hancock include *The Loyalists of Revolutionary Delaware* (1977); *Liberty and Independence: The History of Delaware during the American Revolution* (1976); *The History of Kent County* (1976), and *The History of Sussex County* (1976) as well as articles in *Delaware History.* Recently he has been studying the legislative history of the period in the process of writing an introduction to the proceedings of the House of Assembly for volumes being edited by Dr. Claudia Bushman, Elizabeth Moyne Homsey, and himself.

In chapter one, probate records, including inventories, in the Delaware State Archives and newpapers in the Historical Society of Delaware were helpful. On black history, see Helen B. Stewart, "The Negro in Delaware to 1829" (University of Delaware, M.A.) and H. Clay Reed, "The Negro in Delaware: Legal Status," in *Delaware: A History of the First State*. 2: 571-580. A study written with much understanding is John A. Munroe, "The Negro in Delaware," *South Atlantic Quarterly*, 56: 428-444 (1951). Dr. Hancock has collected material on black history, which is yet unpublished. On social life, see Leon deValinger, Jr., and Virginia E. Shaw, eds., *A Calendar of Ridgely Family Letters, 1742-1899*, 1 (1948). Some interesting miscellaneous items in the Ridgely Collection in the Delaware State Archives are not included in the printed volumes. On social life, see William P. Frank and Harold Hancock, "Caesar Rodney's Two Hundred and Fiftieth Anniversary: An Evaluation," *Delaware History*, 18: 63-76 and William P. Frank, *Caesar Rodney: Patriot: Delaware's Hero for All Times and All Seasons* (1976). On the life of women, see Barbara Clark Smith, *After the Revolution: The Smithsonian History of Everyday Life in the Eighteenth Century* (1985). Laura Gehringer presents interesting material about eighteenth century life in "A Statistical Study of 1797 Kent County Tax Assessments" (MS). See also Madeline Dunn Hite, "A Profile of Kent County, Delaware, 1780-1800" (MS) which examines life at the end of the eighteenth century using a variety of sources.

Dr. Bernard Herman has written several articles on housing and architecture of the period and has a forthcoming book which covers a wider expanse of time. See his *Coastwatch* essay on eighteenth century housing in Sussex County entitled "History on the Move" in May 1985; the chapter entitled "Delaware Vernacular: Folk Housing in Three Counties," in Camille Wells, ed., *Perspectives in Vernacular Architecture* (1982); and his scholarly essay "Architectural Renewal and the Maintenance of Customary Relationships," which will appear in a special issue of *Western Folklore Quarterly*. In 1987 the University of Tennessee will publish his book entitled *Architecture and Rural Life in Central Delaware: 1700–1900*.

On the chapter on agriculture, I consulted the Tilton notes, newspapers, Rodney material, and articles written by Dr.

Bernard Herman, *supra*. See also his essay entitled "The Objects of Discourse: Evidence and Method in Material Culture Study and Agricultural History" to be published in a forthcoming volume entitled *North American Material Culture Research* by the Institute of Social Economic Research, Memorial University of Newfoundland. On the life of farmers, see Smith, *supra*. Lynn Ellen Peterson presents interesting material in a manuscript essay entitled "A Rural Economy and a System of Exchange in Kent County, Delaware."

On manufacturing, in addition to the studies by Dr. Munroe, I consulted P.C. Welsh, "The Brandywine Mills: A Chronicle of Industry, 1762-1816," *Delaware History* 7: 17-36; "Wilmington Merchants, Millers and Ocean Ships: The Components of an Early Industrial Town," *Delaware History, 7:* 319-336 (1957); and Sara G. Farris, "Wilmington's Maritime Commerce, 1775-1807," *Delaware History,* 14: 22-51 (1970). See also Eugene Ferguson, *Oliver Evans, Inventive Genius of the American Industrial Revolution* (1980). Articles by James M. Tunnell, Jr., on the salt and iron industries in Sussex County appeared in *Delaware History* in volumes 4 and 6 respectively. On papermaking, see Harold B. Hancock and Norman B. Wilkinson, "The Gilpins and their Endless Papermaking Machine," *Pennsylvania Magazine of History and Biography,* 57 (1947): 391-405.

On towns see Carol E. Hoffecker, *Brandywine Village: The Story of a Milling Community* (1974); Anna T. Lincoln, *Wilmington Delaware—Three Centuries under Four Flags* (1937); Constance Cooper, "A Town among Cities: New Castle, Delaware, 1780–1840," (University of Delaware, Ph.D., 1983); Jeannette Eckman, *New Castle on the Delaware* (1936; revised by Anthony Higgins in 1973); Joseph R. Lake, *Hockessin: A Pictorial History* (1976); and Richard R. Cooch, *History of Christiana, Delaware* (1976). Useful material was found in Dick Carter's history of Sussex County and also in Dr. Hancock's histories of Kent County and of Sussex County.

On transportation, helpful material was located in travel

books and newspapers, and also in the Rodney, Clowes, and Corbit manuscripts in the Historical Society of Delaware.

On education, see Lyman P. Powell, *The History of Education in Delaware* (1893), which has not yet been superseded, although it is almost one hundred years old. Margaret Kane's dissertation on public education was helpful. See also *The Friends School in Wilmington* (1948); "The Minutes of the Wilmington Academy, 1777-1802," *Delaware History*, 3: 181-226 (1949); C. L. Reese Jr., ed., "Some Reminiscences of Wilm't'n and my Youthful Days—by John Hamilton," *Delaware History*, 1: 89-98 (1946); and Whitfield J. Bell, Jr., "Patriot-Improvers: Some Early Members of the American Philosophical Society," *Delaware History*, 11: 195-207 (1966), as well as the autobiography of William Morgan, *supra*.

On religion, I found refreshing and illuminating William H. Williams, *The Garden of Methodism: The Delmarva Peninsula, 1679-1820* (1985). See also E. C. Hallman, *The Garden of Methodism* (1948); Allen B. Clark and Jane Herson, *New Light on Old Barratt's: A History of Barratt's Chapel* (1984); Frank Zebley, *The Churches of Delaware* (1947); M. Catherine Downing, *Sydenham Thorne, Clergyman and Founder* (1974); Kenneth L. Carroll, *Joseph Nichols and the Nicholites: A Look at the "New Quakers" of Maryland, Delaware, North and South Carolina* (1962) and his article entitled "Joseph Nichols of Delaware: An Eighteenth Century Religious Leader," *Delaware History*, 7: 37-48 (1956); Richard B. Cook, *The Early and Later Delaware Baptists* (1880); Morgan Edwards, "Materials towards a History of the Baptists in the Delaware State," *Pennsylvania Magazine of History and Biography*, 9: 45-61; Nelson W. Rightmyer, *The Anglican Church in Delaware* (1947); and Elizabeth Waterston, *Churches in Delaware during the Revolution* (1925).

On the ratification of the Constitution, I consulted Dr. John A. Munroe, *supra;* Leon deValinger, Jr., *How Delaware Became the First State* (1974); George H. Ryden, *Delaware—The First State in the Union* (1938); and the sections of Reed's history written by Jeannette Eckman. Dr. Hancock has made a special study of Delaware's action for inclusion in a chapter of a book on the ratification process in the thirteen original states. Material relating to Delaware's ratification has been conveniently arranged from original dcuments, newspapers, and letters in Merrill Jensen, *The Documentary History of the Ratification of the Constitution,* vol. 3 (1978).

INDEX